DEAD RECKONINGS

A Review of Horror and the Weird in the Arts
Edited by Alex Houstoun and Michael J. Abolafia

No. 24 (Fall 2018)

DEAD RECKONINGS is published by Hippocampus Press, P.O. Box 641, New York, NY 10156 (www.hippocampuspress.com). Copyright © 2018 by Hippocampus Press. Cover art by Jason C. Eckhardt. Cover design by Barbara Briggs Silbert. Hippocampus Press logo by Anastasia Damianakos. Orders and subscriptions should be sent to Hippocampus Press. Contact Alex Houstoun at deadreckoningsjournal@gmail.com for assignments or before submitting a publication for review.

ISSN 1935-6110
ISBN 978-1-61498-234-0

A Feast in Small Bites

Géza A. G. Reilly

ROBERT AICKMAN. *Compulsory Games*. Edited by Victoria Nelson. New York: New York Review Books, 2018. xvii, 368 pp. $17.95 tpb. ISBN: 978-1-68137-189-4.

I don't want to like the writing of Robert Aickman.

That might seem to be a strange way to start a review, but it is nevertheless true. Whenever I sit down to read some of Aickman's work, such as the 2018 edition of *Compulsory Games* published by New York Review Books, I inevitably have the same sense of unease that I experience when I sit down to read Thomas Ligotti's writing. Aickman's short stories invariably have the effect of instilling in the reader distrust in the solidity of the world, and I cannot say that I enjoy such a sensation. To be fair to Aickman, his stories are far less depressing than Thomas Ligotti's, but that doesn't make the hinge by which they operate any less unsettling.

The comparison to Ligotti is equally valid in the execution of Aickman's stories. Few authors are as capable of creating exquisite prose pieces where every sentence adds upon the last in furtherance of an increasing quality of dislocation from the prosaic world. That dislocation seems to be the point behind Aickman's stories over and against any rigid mechanics of plot, and we are often left with denouements where a sense of meaning is ever retreating. The various worlds in Aickman's stories are often cruel ones where human logic maintains a hold only by the very tips of its fingernails. An eruption of the unreal might enter at any time, for any reason, and leave little more in its wake than chaos.

That chaos is inimical to Aickman's kind of protagonist. Whether women or men, they all seem to be an ideal of 'the common person.' They are usually working- or middle-class, burdened with the sorts of everyday problems that make them instantly relatable. Their prosaic lives slip away quickly, however, due to the aforementioned eruption of impossible elements. Although not every single story in *Compulsory Games* ends up in death or degradation, many of them do, and the ones that do not (barring the subdued exception of "A Disciple of Plato") still find their conclusions in the dislocation of the normal expectations of life.

To the best of my ability to tell, the stories in *Compulsory Games* are either never before collected or rarely collected. With some of the stories, the reason why is fairly obvious: "The Coffin House" and "The Fully-Conducted Tour," for example, feel unfinished, with the former especially coming across as a fragment of what could have been an excellent story. There is no overarching theme to the collection per se, outside of Aickman "open[ing] a door [. . .] and, at the end, leav[ing] it open," as Victoria Nelson states in her introduction. For the aficionado of horror, perhaps the most interesting stories would be the exceptionally weird "Wood" or the delicate "Le Miroir," though I firmly think that the stand-outs in an Aickman collection depend entirely on the tastes of the individual reader. For me, the highlights of the collection were "No Time Is Passing" and the titular "Compulsory Games"—perhaps because it is in these stories that the slide into absolute chaos is most pronounced—though it must be said that "Just a Song at Twilight" stands out in my memory as creating a creeping dread that I have not felt in some time.

Every one of the fifteen stories in *Compulsory Games*, fragmentary or not, does, as stated, possess Aickman's customary quality. There is a purposefulness, a finesse, to Aickman's writing in even the most bizarre of contexts that puts to shame the clumsier efforts of other authors. This is, in part, why Aickman is lauded so heavily in editor Victoria Nelson's "Introduction: Under the Skin." However, Nelson is also strangely hostile to the weird and horror communities who have helped keep Aickman's work in print. Indeed, she wants Aickman's stories to escape being "locked in the Gothic cellar" as though it were somehow terrible for his collections to be shelved alongside other classics of genre. This is a standard complaint about purportedly 'genre' texts, and it is one I will never understand.

After all, it is the case that 'genre' is little more than a classification system that we have created to bring order to a sea of texts. Readerly expectation and authorial intention blend together (sometimes in unbalanced proportions) to *create* genre. Nevertheless, some commentators persist in thinking that there is a superior tier of so-called 'literary' fiction below which resides everything that can be neatly categorized into a genre. This is a ridiculous notion, and it is frankly irresponsible (not to mention insulting) for Nelson to suggest that Aickman's popularity in the "fantasy fandom world" condemns it to being passed over by "the more literary reader." The sooner we are able to move past this idea that there is a gulf between 'literary' and 'genre' texts (as opposed to simply being comfortable saying that one does not enjoy certain texts), the better.

Can I safely say that *Compulsory Games* is the sort of text that many readers will be comfortable with? No, sadly not. Other critics might say that Aickman's writing is only for the more discerning reader, but I think that is gilding the lily somewhat. The fact of the matter is that Robert Aickman appeals to a wide swath of readers—scholars, fans, and others alike. But people can only know if they fall into that swath by dipping their toes into Aickman. *Compulsory Games* is certainly one of the better ways to find out if Aickman is for you. I don't *want* to like the work of Robert Aickman, just as I don't want to like the work of Thomas Ligotti. But I do, and I recommend them both, even if it is only for one proverbial taste-test. *Compulsory Games* may not be a feast in comparison to other Aickman collections, but it is certainly enough to chew on for a while.

Alive with Darkness

S. T. Joshi

RAMSEY CAMPBELL. *By the Light of My Skull*. Hornsea, UK: PS Publishing, 2018. 294 pp. £20.00 trade hc; £40.00 slipcased hc. ISBN 978-178636-330-5
RAMSEY CAMPBELL. *The Way of the Worm*. Hornsea, UK: PS Publishing, 2018. £20.00 trade hc; £40.00 slipcased hc. ISBN 978-786363-59-6.

An historian once referred to Mozart as "an undeserved gift to humanity." I don't know what we lowly mortals have done to deserve not one, but two new works by Ramsey Campbell, published more or less simultaneously, but it is a gift that no devotee of weird fiction is likely to reject.

By the Light of My Skull is Campbell's first short story collection since *Visions from Brichester* (2015); and since that volume consisted largely of Campbell's early Lovecraftian tales, we have to go back to 2013 for his last collection of recent tales, *Holes for Faces.* In the past five years, Campbell has clearly devoted the bulk of his attention to novels; but the fifteen stories in this new volume make unmistakably clear that he remains a master of the short form.

What distinguishes Campbell's work, whether it be novels or tales, is his unerring focus on exactly those scenarios that make us fearful and uneasy. His keen insight into human character allows him to zero in on the troubling aspects of domestic life, social life, and our very place in an uncaring universe.

Many stories in *By the Light of My Skull* deal with familial breakdowns that are all too familiar to us. Hence we have "Find My Name," in which a grandmother struggles to protect her infant grandson from the clutches of his derelict father; "Reading the Signs," in which a man driving in the dark picks up a man and a small boy who may or may not be his son; and "The Moons," where some teenagers on a beach are threatened by a gang of older teenagers. In each case, the story veers from the very real dangers we all face on a daily basis into the supernatural, in a way that only enhances the undercurrent of terror.

It is interesting to note how many of these stories feature protagonists who are either elderly (usually a long-married couple) or are teenagers. Campbell, himself now a venerable seventy-two, can no doubt draw upon his own experiences in the former group of tales—and, by the way of his children, perhaps in the latter group as well, even though his son and daughter are well beyond their teenage years. The frustration latent in living in a time of rapid technological change is highlighted in "Know Your Code," where both members of an elderly couple are perplexed by all the codes one now needs to recall to activate credit cards, ATMs, and other devices.

"The Callers" is one of the most unnerving of Campbell's recent tales, where a teenage boy blunders into a bingo parlor where his grandmother is playing. Can it be that the other players—almost all of them elderly women—are actually making sexual advances on the boy? What could their intentions possibly be when they approach his house, chanting esoterically? "The Impression" also deals with a teenage boy and his grandmother, who visit the ruins of a nobleman's estate to secure a rubbing from his sarcophagus. The gradual accumulation of ghostly details makes this tale a masterwork.

"Fetched" deals with a retired couple, Laurence and Violet, who seek to find a locale from Laurence's childhood. It has now become an exclusive development, and the couple face anomalous hostility from the residents. A poster of a missing dog becomes omnipresent—and leads to an unthinkable denouement. In "The Page" another retired couple, Ewen and Joyce, are vacationing on one of the Greek islands (another island serves as the setting of Campbell's recent novel *Thirteen Days by Sunset Beach*), where Ewen finds the final page of an apparently self-published novel by a writer who used to live on the island. The author's daughter says her father is dead—but is he really so, so long as even a single copy of his book survives?

The bittersweet poignancy of aging is expressed in a different manner in "On the Tour," focusing on a man in Liverpool named Stu Stewart, whose only claim to fame is that he was a member of a band that had played with the Beatles during their early days, and whose talents as a drummer were apparently lauded by Ringo Starr. Stu becomes obsessed with what the leader of a tour group is saying about him as it passes by his building. This superb exercise in paranoia is tinged with pathos for a man's clinging to his one brief moment of celebrity. "The Fun of the Fair" is affecting in a different way. The tale's avowed plot deals with a widow, Elaine, who digs up a wooden horse in her garden and finds that her property had once served as the locale for what Campbell calls a "roundabout" (what we in the US would call a merry-go-round); she also learns that the owner of the fairground had died in a fire while in a mirror maze. But these events, unsettling as they are, also underscore Elaine's own heartbreak at losing her husband, Nigel.

"The Watched" is one of the more elaborate stories in the book, vividly etching the social decay brought on by poverty and drugs. Its protagonist is a twelve-year-old boy, Jimmy Cooper, who is approached by a policeman, a man named Blundell, whose daughter has recently died; Blundell blames the Dibbin family, living next door to Jimmy, who are drug dealers. But then Jimmy learns that Blundell is no longer on the force—and also learns that the entire Dibbin family has perished in a nearby canal. Blundell also died there—but Jimmy learns that the policeman's relentless pursuit of his perceived enemies may not be over.

And we cannot bypass "Her Face," where a young boy, Joe, thinks that a Halloween mask he sees in a store run by a domineering old woman, Mrs. Dillard, is of Mrs. Dillard herself—and is perhaps more than a mask. The tale concludes with an incredibly potent encounter between Joe and an old woman wearing that same mask.

Now we move on to *The Way of the Worm*. This triumphant conclusion of a Lovecraftian trilogy that began with *The Searching Dead* (2016) and continued with *Born to the Dark* (2017) will be deeply satisfying to all devotees of weird fiction, Lovecraftian fiction, Campbellian fiction, and anyone who relishes witnessing a virtuoso of his craft performing at the top of his form. If, as is fitting, these three novels are regarded as a single entity, they unquestionably rank near the very top of Campbell's literary output—a difficult achievement indeed, since his array of scintillating novels and tales far surpasses that of every other weird writer of the past fifty years, and perhaps every writer in the entire history of weird fiction.

A warning, however: in *The Way of the Worm* Campbell feels no inclination to supply any kind of synopsis of the two previous novels, under the sensible expectation that only those who have digested those works can fully appreciate this final installment. In those two books we have seen Dominic Sheldrake of Liverpool advance from his teenage years in the 1950s (*The Searching Dead*) to a somewhat unstable marriage in the 1980s with a woman named Lesley and a five-year-old son, Toby (*Born to the Dark*). Now we reach the present day, where Dominic, in his seventies, is facing multiple trials and tribulations—not the least of them the death of his beloved wife. Toby is now married to a woman named Claudine; and the moment we learn this we are alarmed, for Claudine was one of the children in a facility called Safe To Sleep organized by the baleful Christian Noble (who, as one of Dominic's teachers in school, inspired vague fear in him and his young friends for his interest in the occult) along with his daughter, Tina, and her son, Christopher. Much of *The Searching Dead* was involved in increasingly frenzied efforts by Dominic—as well as his compatriots Jim Bailey (a policeman) and Roberta (Bobby) Parkin (a journalist)—in exposing the nefariousness of the Nobles. Even though *Born to the Dark* ended with the apparent destruction of the Safe To Sleep facility, we are hardly reassured that the danger represented by the Nobles is in any way over.

And, indeed, it is not. Both Dominic and the reader are distressed to find that the Nobles are now the leaders of a church or cult called the Church of the Eternal Three—suspiciously similar to the Trinity Church of the Spirit whose building Dominic and his cohorts (who have long called themselves the Tremendous Three) set ablaze in *The Searching Dead*. Christian Noble must now be incredibly old, but he and his daughter and grandson are still thriving. What's more, Toby and Claudine are now members of the church, as are many other former patients of Safe To Sleep; still more disturbingly, Dominic's son and his wife are even inculcating their five-year-old daughter, Macy, into the church.

But is it possible that the church is really benign? Toby does his best to persuade his father of that, and some of the keenest moments of tension in *The Way of the Worm* focus on intense discussions between Toby (who is clearly sincere in his belief that the church has benefited his family) and Dominic, who knows all too well that the Nobles are anything but benevolent. Campbell may well be underscoring the dangers of religious brainwashing here: he himself has long struggled with the Catholicism he was forced to absorb as a child, and there is a clear implication of his disapproval of any sort of brainwashing of the young before they are mentally and emotionally ready to decide matters for themselves. The fact that the names of both of the churches established by the Nobles have unquestionably Catholic resonances underscores this point.

What the members of the Church of the Eternal Three seem to be engaging in is a series of deep meditation sessions—and what could be the harm in that? When Dominic grudgingly agrees to participate in such a session—which, to his alarm, takes place in the very building, Starview Towers, where Toby and his family live—he appears to dredge up memories of when he was a newborn baby. That is bad enough, but it is at this point that Dominic learns that the church is led by one Christopher Le Bon—which he easily recognizes as an anagram for Noble. Later, Dominic attends a sermon by the entire Noble family, where Christopher delivers an ominous sermon about the imminent return of chaos to the world:

> "Alliances are breaking up across the world. . . . Continents are separating into countries, and countries are splitting apart too. There are wars and rumours of more wars, and unseen armies fighting for no country are at large all around us. Religions are reverting to their primitive states, and madness is loose on the streets, and ruling country after country. The climate is returning to its birth. Gender grows more fluid, and the minds of the masses are gathering in the space their computers and electronic devices create."

There is more, but this is enough to show how Campbell has deftly weaved our current sociopolitical troubles into a tapestry of supernatural menace.

The novel gains dynamism when Dominic uses his phone to record a private conversation among the Nobles in which Christian essentially admits the appalling fact that he himself begat Christopher through an incestuous union with his own daughter. Dominic passes on the tape to Bobby, who writes a blog about it. A furor erupts, and the Nobles are arrested. In a subsequent trial, Christopher is found guilty of incest—but, to the astonishment and dismay of Dominic and others, his ten-year sentence is suspended, and the Nobles calmly walk out of the courtroom. This whole episode is narrated with such compelling intensity—including gripping cross-examinations of both Bobby and Dominic by the Nobles' attorney—that the reader comes to believe that Campbell could easily have excelled at courtroom dramas if he had not (thankfully for readers of weird fiction) chosen to work in another genre.

Throughout this whole segment, Dominic is pained by the obviously sincere disappointment of Toby and his wife at what he has done to the Nobles; Dominic, in turn, is crestfallen that his own son could be so indifferent to the Nobles' sexual irregularities, to say nothing of other, more anomalous dangers they present, of which he has first-hand knowledge. When Dominic accedes to another meditation session, he actually envisions his own death. Toby blandly remarks, "It's your future that's remembering."

But worse things are in store for Dominic. He is already battered by age, ill health, the death of his wife, and now an agonizing estrangement from his own son and grandchild. When the Nobles are leaving the courtroom, Christopher comes up to him and states forebodingly, "You're starting to live in our world. . . . You will until you die. . . . And then so much more." Dominic realizes he must take more decisive action to thwart the Nobles. Finding out where they live, he sees their house as he is traveling on a ferry: they appear to be "dancing rapidly back and forth . . . describing an intricate sinuous series of patterns with their entire body." And is it possible that their faces have all merged together? "A single face could never have filled all the windows of the house, glaring out at me with its six monstrously enlarged eyes, bereft of pupils but alive with darkness."

But others seem to do the work he had set out to do. A gang of citizens, outraged at the outcome of the trial, set the Nobles' house ablaze. The Nobles, apparently naked, burn to death: "I thought I saw their bodies start not just to melt but to merge into a single monstrous shape." But the entire course of the trilogy has led us to discount the possibility that the Nobles could be so easily dispensed with. Toby accuses his own father of complicity in the arson ("you've got rid of Christian and his family")—and he blandly takes over leadership of the church. He also posts online the pages from Christian Noble's journals that Dominic had copied out as a teenager. Dominic is disturbed by the parallels: on the one hand Christian, Tina, and Christopher Noble; on the other hand, Toby, Claudine, and Macy. When, after an argument, Claudine peremptorily declares that Dominic is no longer welcome in her house, Dominic seems to have reached the end of his rope.

There is much more to *The Way of the Worm* than the menace of the Nobles and the familial tension between Dominic and his son. Subsequent events, directly or indirectly engineered by the hideous entity that the Nobles have now become, cause Dominic to be bereft of nearly all his friends and family; and yet, even this is not the worst fate that befalls him. In a climax that melds otherworldly, cosmic horror with the distinctively intimate tragedy in which Dominic finds himself enmeshed, Campbell unifies his own worldview with Lovecraft's—and at the same time shows that richly detailed and loving characterizations of the human protagonists not only are not a barrier to the expression of cosmic insignificance, but can actually enhance it by rendering more poignant the fates of the hapless human beings who fall into the clutches of those forces (i.e., the Nobles) who symbolize cosmic dread.

One of the most striking elements of *The Way of the Worm* is the manner in which it features a pervasive sense of *unease*. Campbell recognizes that *fear* is difficult to maintain over the length of the novel; it is too intense an emotion for the human psyche to endure for a prolonged period. But unease can be manipulated by the skillful writer in ways that become almost as unbearable as brute fear, but that can nonetheless be sustained almost without cessation. In this novel, Campbell also creates the novelty of *dialogue* that enhances the sense of unease, as featured in verbal sparring between Dominic and Christian Noble, among others. In the hands of lesser writers such colloquies can seem corny or contrived, but Campbell uses repartée not only to forward the plot but to underscore the deeply sinister threat that the Nobles constitute to the peace and safety of the world.

I have little doubt that Ramsey Campbell's trilogy—for the three novels must be regarded as a tightly knit unity—will take its place among the stellar accomplishments in the realm of weird fiction. I struggle to find any trio of novels in our field that could match its achievement—an achievement that extends not merely to its deft portrayal of numerous characters over six decades and the impeccable elegance and mellifluousness of its prose, but above all to the grimly terrifying nature of its weird manifestations. It is too early to say that this trilogy is the summit of Campbell's achievement, for he (unlike his protagonist, Dominic Sheldrake) remains a vigorous septuagenarian, with much more work to come in the future; but readers, critics, and literary historians will have little hesitation in regarding it as a landmark that few of his rivals could hope to match.

God Is a Disease: The Mystic Exile of Andrzej Zulawski's *Possession*

Nathan Chazan

Exile is a spiritual condition. Our homes mold our understanding of ourselves, and in the denial of places we are forced to reform our understanding of identity. This rupture turns the thinker inwards toward profound emotion while imbuing exterior observations with cosmic distance. Exile and departure arguably form the foundation of Judeo-Christian faith, with Genesis positing our human condition to be a consequence of banishment from Eden. Vilém Flusser, perhaps unwittingly, acknowledges the religious significance of exile in the deeply personal opening statements of *The Challenge of the Migrant:* "I am a Jew, and the adage 'next year in Jerusalem' accompanied me through childhood" (1).

Yet exile is not so much a state of movement as it is a state of enclosure. Exiles may be forcibly removed from their homeland, but the experience of that removal is the pointed awareness of that place to which they have arrived, an acute sensation of dwelling (or boundaries) emerging from anti-dwelling. Expulsion from a space creates awareness of that space. Consider Heidegger's definition of a boundary from his essay "Building Dwelling Thinking":

> A boundary is not that at which something stops but, as the Greeks recognized, the boundary is that from which something begins its essential unfolding. [. . .] Space is that for which room has been made, that which is let into its bounds. (332)

Could personal experiences function like the spaces of Heidegger's boundary, formed by definitions of absence? Heidegger's spaces are of course not merely places but dwellings, loci where one perceives oneself as existing or being. Heidegger states that the dilemma faced by mortals is that they "must ever search anew for the essence of dwelling, that they must ever learn to dwell" (339). Although Heidegger often plays on nostalgic strains of embodied places lost (the Black Forest lodge, for example), it is perhaps worth considering expulsion as creating a definition for one's dwelling just as four walls create the parameters for a room to exist. In the loss of a place, one becomes conscious of where one is and where one has been. When one can say "I cannot go back there" one acknowledges at once where one is and where one has been. Despair, depression, and dysphoria are themselves articulations of one's awareness of embodiment (cf. Heidegger: "Indeed, the loss of rapport with things that occurs in states of depression would be wholly impossible if even such a state were not still what it is as a human state: that is, a staying with things" [335]). Thus, expulsion itself implies the creation of enclosure, a pulling in rather than a kicking out.

Andrzej Zulawski's film *Possession* (1981) was born of a revelatory experience of enclosure. The genesis of the film came in exile, of a literal, creative, and emotional nature. Following the seizure of his epic *On the Silver Globe* (*Na Srebrnym Globie,* completed in 1989) by the Polish government in 1979, Zulawski found himself unable to work in his home country, effectively banned from Poland. Leaving the country also brought an end to his marriage to the actress Małgorzata Braunek, a longtime partner both creative and romantic. Zulawski found himself in New York, contemplating suicide, but chose to live (in some accounts, it was none other than Andy Warhol who talked him out of killing himself). Zulawski's replacement for death was *Possession,* the script for which Zulawski wrote compulsively and rapidly over the course of days following his abandoned attempt to die (Jazowska).

The genesis of *Possession* is an essential prehistory to the film, not because a biographical reading is necessary (although parallels to Zulawski's life certainly make themselves known when sought), but because the place of its creation better locates the film's mystical quality. The concept of the movie *Possession* came from a man writing in a state of emptiness, removed from the people, places, things, and communities that composed his connection to being in the world. Dwelling in what must have been one of those truly shabby New York apartments of legend, Andrzej Zulawski, a man who had, in a sense, already died once, pours all his experiences into a blueprint for a movie until the personal becomes a window into the multifaceted universal, and even a little further, toward some unvoiceable unknown. This is an auteurist myth, an imaginary version of "Andrzej Zulawski" probably both dishonest to the man and to the movie he wrote and directed, but it is a helpful myth to hold on to while wading through *Possession,* a film that (as my friend Alex Lugo once claimed) "remolds a bit of your soul while you watch it."

Possession opens on images of the Berlin wall, accompanied by a brief, imposing shot of a wooden cross. These images are deliberate, as they encapsulate two of the film's key obsessions—location and God, entrapment and infinity. This pairing is not an opposition; enclosure in space is what coaxes out the gesture to the unknown, the desire to see something else and the abject terror of that other melded in madness and inspiration. Carine Varene writes eloquently on Berlin's role in the film:

> From the very first frames, anecdotal reality is out of the equation. Berlin is a different city. The boundaries of the possible have been broken. The past and unspoken history of the place gives a strange weight to the film, an internal anxiety. The set lends itself to a mystical experience: it is an enclosed environment, the streets are deserted, the city is inhabited only by a concrete divide, symbolic of a painful reality. (70)

The "reality" Varene speaks of could be Zulawski's exile; or, rather, the Berlin wall becomes a thing imbued with some sensation between the separation anxieties of the film's characters and those of the film's director. The wall, a sign of enclosure and the inability to leave, is omnipresent—the majority of the locations in the film hug right up to it. In *Possession,* it is impossible to look out the window of any building without seeing the wall, and upon the wall there is probably someone in military fatigues looking back. While Berlin as a generic cultural milieu is irrelevant to the film, the form of the city is essential to the closed, manic space *Possession* creates.

Possession is a film of confounding place, lacking a real nationality—a French-financed production conceived by an exiled Polish man, filmed in West Berlin, starring a New Zealander (Sam Neill), a Frenchwoman (Isabelle Adjani), and an assortment of Germans (Heinz Bennent, Margit Carstensen, Carl Duering; recognizable faces from films by Bergman, Fassbinder, and Kubrick, respectively). Although Adjani was certainly the most famous name associated with the film during its making, every actor in *Possession* (with the notable exception of Sam Neill) was an internationally exportable name in the art-house market of its time. The cast of *Possession* also shares another notable trait, again with the sole exception of Neill—English is not their first language. But *Possession* is an English-language film, written in a room in New York; this international language as spoken by non-natives is the film's most discernable nationality. (A French dub of the film exists, but Zulawski has dismissed this version as inessential [Bird and Thrower 34].) Andrei Tarkovsky once described *Possession* as a film with no meaning other than "money, money, money . . . Nothing real, nothing true" (324). Tarkovsky's condemnation to the film seems to this author strange and colored by an ascription of a mythical, irrelevant Americanism to the work, but he is not wrong to see the film as written in the language of commerce if only on a purely literal, unaesthetic level.

Sam Neill's Mark is thus the only character in the film who is comfortable speaking the English language, and is thus the only person in the film with command of the space he inhabits, what one might call authority or the power of reason. Yet as the only clean speaker of the language, Mark is marked as the only foreigner in the film, the outsider to a space of incomprehension. Mark is a secret agent, a job that evokes the seductive imperialism of the James Bond cycle, but outside this fantastic profession there is discomfort and confusion, the man violently rocking in a chair and staring vacantly. Mark's home is not his nationality; his wife and son are unknown to him. The pretense of linguistic comfort betrays Mark's spiritual lack, a need to either find meaning or destroy speech.

If Sam Neill has the cleanest English in the film, Isabelle Adjani's is the strangest, oddly inflected and heavily accented.

Adjani's performance as Anna is extreme and excessive; every syllable screamed and howled, an evolution of Zulawski's revelatory philosophy of acting ("Acting is the victory of ugliness over the beauty of the world!" proclaims a character in *On the Silver Globe*), often described as hysterical, although schizophrenia would be a more accurate and less misogynist analogy. But the rhythm of Anna's strange pronouncements also carry in them Adjani's own struggles with the English language (Bird and Thrower 34–36)—in many scenes, it is likely that Adjani may not actually understand the words that she is saying. Anna is a woman possessed—by Mark her estranged husband, by her lover Heinrich (Heinz Bennent), by the Lovecraftian monster she cares for sexually, and perhaps by God or the devil—yet her ultimate possession is by her own voice, streaming emphatically out of the vessel of actress Adjani. Wandering nomadically between Mark's apartment and the monster's, Anna is rooted neither in location nor language, and with nothing else to turn to approaches ecstasy that some might call divine revelation, others mental illness.

The characters of *Possession* are struggling with internal ailments linked in part to a detachment from place, anguish that surpasses description and can only be approached through contact with inhuman extremity. The same could be said about the twelfth-century Christian mystic, composer, and polymath St. Hildegard of Bingen. Hildegard was given to the church by her destitute family around the age of ten, placed in the care of the anchoress Jutta, "a woman who voluntarily took last rites and entered a vault [. . .] from which she was never to emerge" (Hickam, foreword to *Selections from Her Writings* viii). Torn from her family, Hildegard became immersed in the spiritual teachings of a woman in confinement. And she did learn well, becoming an influential authority and elected leader of her convent, expanding her world substantially by the time of her entrapped mentor's passing. Hildegard experienced illnesses that made her body become suddenly weak and experience fiery visions, visions that she would come to interpret as messages to her from God. Like Zulawski's multifaceted exile, Hildegard's life is marked by ruptures in her environment, relationships, and physical temperament that became a source of artistic inspiration and mystical revelation.

In a letter to Elisabeth of Schoenau, Hildegard vividly describes the aftermath of original sin as a powerful lesson in the mutability of consciousness (*Lectiones* 103): "omnia elementa implicuerunt se in vicissitudinem luminis et tenebrarum" ("all the elements entangled themselves amid the alteration of lights and shadows" [translation mine]). Hildegard invokes a world physically altered and twisting in response to a sensational change. The shifting terrain of the sinful world could be understood both as an emotional change or a change in place. This phenomenological ambiguity applies to the corresponding biblical story of Genesis, in which man cannot remain in the garden because of a change in his nature. Unlike the Old Testament account, Hildegard's allegory does not require bodily departure to take place for dwelling to be lost or changed. Indeed, perception is key to Hildegard's "vicissitudinem luminis et tenebrarum"—the world becomes different perhaps because of man's new temperament, but the agent of this difference is lighting, new contrasts bringing new forms into view.

Like Hildegard's remolded world, the places of *Possession* embody exile, although they are never left—indeed, it may be impossible for the film's protagonists to leave. Instead, all the elements entangle themselves in reflection of departure and absence. Contrasts of light and color signify changes of state in *Possession*. Where our medieval mystics balance brightness and darkness as oppositions in conceiving of society, *Possession* presents us with two ranges of hues, blue and greenish-yellow. The blue has a pale purity, either soft or sterile but somehow welcoming, almost submissive to the eye. The blue is deepest on Anna's dress, lightest in the apartment she and Mark share, the cool light of the hallway almost voicing her absence. The yellow-greens are a harsher color, bile-like. The color field evokes illness and oblivion from its first appearance, when Mark wakes up in a room not his own, unaware of himself, drenched in sweat. He cannot recognize himself at first, and neither could I, when first viewing the film—Sam Neill wears a beard that changes his character's appearance greatly, and the light makes him that much more alien to us.

The two colors are not light and darkness—for such an anguished work, *Possession* is a film strikingly bereft of dark, a frightening film in its clarity. However, blue and yellow-green clearly embody two states. Mark's house and the world he lives in are blue places, Anna's apartment with the monster is full of the sick yellows. We could call blue Mark's controlled, normative world, and yellow-green the unbalanced, psychotic world of Anna's unknown life. We could then call the blue "good" or "light," and the yellow-green "evil," "darkness." There is certainly a satanic monster dwelling in the green, and by the end of the film that monster is completed as Mark's great impostor, a green-eyed man. But definitions are not so easy to ascribe to *Possession,* and morals even less so. The first sight of yellow places Mark centrally in it, and Anna's dress remains the bluest focal point. Zulawski calls blue "the color of rejection" and yellow "the color of passion," citing Goethe and Sufi mysticism as inspiration (Bird and Thrower 44). Is the journey from blue to yellow one from night into day, a cruel awakening into re-embodied life?

Instead of viewing blue and yellow as signifiers of characters or attitudes, they can be considered two ways of seeing whose alteration makes the state of the world experientially different, just as Hildegard's forms twist into each other by the changing balance of the light. It's all in the eyes—like the new Mark, Anna's double, Helen (also portrayed by Isabelle Adjani), has green eyes instead of blue, so by the end of the film the pair experience the world literally through a different lens.

Even the highly moral Christian mystic allows value to be placed on flows in perception as much as static paradigms of goodness and transgression. In a strange letter fragment Hildegard recalls a vision of the first woman's rape, in which "the ancient serpent," penetrating Eve with a penis emerging from his mouth, "spews black fire from his mouth which, afterward, becomes the torment of such pleasure," aware that "mankind would be born sexually through that penis of his shame." The problem of original sin is not sex, but rather shameful sex, the perpetuation of original rape, and those who overcome that shame (through chastity, of course, although

Hildegard seems oddly more euphemistic about this in comparison to her otherwise explicit language in this letter) will:

> Prepare arrows in the quiver, and shoot them with a luminous fire at the serpent's penis, puncturing it with wound in such a way that the serpent is shamed, like a man who knows that he is naked, but cannot cover himself. (*Personal Correspondence* 128–29)

This passage is valuable because it demonstrates a slippery possibility for Judeo-Christian morality, a mutability of shame. Hildegard's response to Satan's dark penis of evil is to envision a penis of light, shooting out the brightness of repentance (or maybe shamelessness) and causing the devil himself to take on our shame as his. It is a triumphant reversal, a new entanglement causing good and evil to refold themselves amid humanity and love. This kind of alteration may be the sort we see in *Possession*.

For many of the cult film enthusiasts who have (for better or for worse) kept the memory of *Possession* alive in American criticism, the film can be reduced to a single sequence, the so-called "subway scene," a virtuoso montage of Anna writhing and howling in anticipation of an explosion of bodily fluid referred to later as a miscarriage. The sequence begins abruptly, a shouting match between Anna and Mark punctured by a jump cut to Anna staring up in silence at Christ on his cross. Holding a bag of groceries to her waist and bobbing a little in awe, Anna begins to moan. A long shot takes Anna out of the church, at which point another jump cut places Anna in the corridor of a subway station, a deep grimy blue space, where immediately awed silence is replaced by violent noise and gesture, divine inspiration made fleshy.

Summaries of this sequence often suggest that Anna is giving birth to the monster, conveniently naming the creature Sister Faith and ascribing it a history, flatly contradicting Anna's own description of the events as a miscarriage—even if she does "have to take care of [her] faith," the product of a miscarriage is by definition not alive. Before the flashback, Anna speaks to Heinrich of two sisters, Faith and Chance, then to Mark she describes a vision of these sisters: "You know these women wrestling in an arena of mud? With their hands locked at each other's throats? Each waiting to see who will die first . . . and both staring at me!" Like a mystic coming to terms with a revelation through allegory, the subway sequence expands on Anna's vision of female wrestlers. The two women are locked in combative unison, and one must fall. This is faith, miscarried at the terminal of transit. What remains is chance, the creature Anna calls unfinished. Later, as Anna makes love to the creature, she cries, "Almost . . . almost." If the creature is to be identified with anyone, it is Sister Chance, not faith. Faith's emergence from Anna is rejected by her environment, while Chance comes from the world, her origins elusive.

Faith is many things, and religious faith is certainly among them, as the sight of Christ suggests. But could faith be associated with dwelling, the faith that one's residence is one's home? Anna is driven out of the church by her ecstasy and loses faith in a place of departure. Anna is then both a prophet and an exile, brilliant in her suffering. Cast out from faith, chance enters Anna's life as the possibility that a new embodied life can be formed in this place that isn't yet home.

Later Christian mystics build on these spatial allegories of spiritual mysteries. Saint Teresa of Avila's great sixteenth-century treatise *The Interior Castle* goes so far as to envision the soul as its own sort of dwelling place, a shining palace that becomes brighter and brighter as one moves deeper inward through seven dwelling places. The bright center of the soul's rooms is at once the most personal and closest to God. Recalling the elements Hildegard pictures as turning inward, the absence of external light pushes humans to seek the light within us. "This castle," says Teresa, "is a creature and the difference therefore between it and God is the same as that between the Creator and his Creature" (284). The human castle is at once a dwelling place, a holy place, and a mortal being.

Professor Daniel Gallagher wrote to me in a private correspondence on the topic of light's recurrence as a spatial theme in Christian mysticism:

The main commonality between Catherine of Siena and Theresa of Avila is their teaching that God brings souls to the consolation they seek by depriving them of light, impeding them of their own efforts to obtain satisfaction by their own powers.

What Gallagher suggests here is that these Christian mystics who speak of light and darkness similarly share an implicit suggestion that darkness is the intended state for our post-Adam man to dwell in. Deprived of the surroundings of heavenly brightness, the soul turns inward to nurture its own inner lights—divine inspiration emerging from the soul. This brings us back to Hildegard's *elementa,* which are bending into themselves. Like the human soul, these *elementa* could be seen as turning inward in contemplation of their self. Although the darkness in Hildegard is the sorrow of exodus, "there might not be 'two' darknesses here. Perhaps [Hildegard] is suggesting that the problem is that humans (and other things?) content themselves with darkness" (Gallagher). Darkness is therefore the absence of light, but not the absence of enlightenment.

A person is assisted in seeing the inner light of divinity when external brightness is stripped away. External darkness could therefore be seen as a rupture in subjective experience. Both Hildegard and Teresa came to their revelations while in states of sudden illness, intense headaches. Writing in the prologue on the difficulties of writing the work, Teresa bemoans: "Such a great noise and weakness in my head that I've found it a hardship even to write concerning necessary business matters" (281). In *Possession*, Mark and Heinrich share an oddly tender exchange on the nature of God:

> HEINRICH: There is nothing to fear except God, whatever that means to you.
> MARK: For me, God is a disease.
> HEINRICH: That's why through a disease we can reach God.

So it is for Teresa and Hildegard. Both experienced intense pains and sicknesses, ailments that we might call migraines or seizures, during which they encountered a version or impression of God. Similarities in their visions (Teresa described her castle to her biographer Fr. Diego de Yepes as "a most beautiful crystal globe like a castle" [Teresa 286], not unlike the elemental orbs that recur in many of Hildegard's visions in *Scivias*) suggest not only theological kinship, but a common experience of a feeling or dysfunction that defies language and normative sensory perception. Teresa's castle is closest to God at the center. If disease strips away a deception by mundane experience that distract from God or truth or our self, then disease is in fact an avenue to God. The headaches of Christian mystics and the exile of Andrzej Zulawski are alike in that the denial of expected experience allows both mystic and director to reach toward the sublime.

The stripping away of routine experience pushes the characters in *Possession* to states of revelation, achieved when barred from their dwellings. This transcendent denial is experienced most vividly by Mark as he attempts to return to his apartment in a sequence that sets off the film's conclusion. As Mark walks casually toward his home, one may find his environment unfamiliar: the symbolic pale blues of Mark's neighborhood have been drained in favor of rich natural-looking daylight, the green of a healthy tree breathing warmth into the frame. In place of the blue are cop cars: Mark cannot enter his home, and a violent confrontation concluding in exploding vehicles confirms this. A virtuoso Steadicam sequence carries Mark through Berlin streets and under brutalist architecture, propelled by motorcycle, dead center in the frame. A scream emerges from Mark, but unlike Anna's ecstatic cries from the subway scene, Mark's voice is a continuous tone, an ambient groan that seems to emit from his body. It is as if something awful is leaving Mark's body—a dispossession.

Mark crashes his motorcycle at the edge of a river steeply bordered by a parking lot. Miraculously, the trashed motorcycle does not fall past the edge of the lot into the river, suggesting a definite spatial boundary, a phenomenal limit, the edge of Mark's world. Like Anna's miscarriage, Mark has been forcibly removed from his normative experience of reality, repelled from his home rather than the symbolic church. The core locations of the film, Mark's apartment and Anna's place with the monster, have been literally exploded by Mark's hands, and as he tears forward he discovers and confirms the contours of his reformed world, the eye of the camera turning toward his being. Mark has found himself: he will literally meet himself in the spiral staircase where he and Anna die. The building containing this staircase is a new place, unseen until this moment but lovingly captured, never viewed from the outside (a scene taking place on the rooftop was included in the script but never shot). Having finally explored the parameters of their new life totally, Mark and Anna enter a truly different place, where Mark's repetition (Mark's double, named by Anna to be the completion of the creature) grants the weary lovers an ending. The game of chance is finished.

The film ends in a new apartment, where Helen, Anna's double, is caring for the child Bob. The apartment is large and spacious with high ceilings, and yet this space's inhabitation looks a bit more snug than Mark's place. The old apartment, full of blue light, seems to push out its dwellers, while Helen's empty, white apartment, full of neutral bright color and negative space, draws its new residents in. Mark's double knocks at the door, and Bob begins to repeat the phrase "Don't open it" to Helen. It may be a warning—the child's voice is full of dread—but the quality of the repetition has more of a magic quality. The boy drones, "Don't oooopen, don't oooopen" as he runs up the stairs and submerges himself in a full bathtub. He looks dead. Earlier in the film, Bob played in the bathtub, fond of breathing underwater. Regardless of Bob's fate, he has assumed his proper place, something he rehearsed for with his nautical games. Bob dwells in the bathtub, transformed into the being his dwelling suggests.

Helen of course goes to the door, but she does not open it, or at least, we don't see her open it. Standing in front of the door, wearing a blank expression that may be terror but may be something else, Helen looks forward while behind her we see the contorted silhouette of Mark's twisted body hugging the window. The sound of bombs are heard. Bob is correct to say "Don't open," not only because Helen should not open the door, but because the door cannot be opened. The film is over. In new personas in a new home, Isabel Adjani and Sam Neill have assumed the perfect positions, an ideal configuration, an image from which nothing new can emerge. Having expressed themselves fully, in harmony with their environment, all can stop. It is a holy image.

What should be grasped from a comparison of mystic authors to Zulawski's film is not linear influence (although Anna is perhaps as inspired by the image of Christ amid her convulsions as Teresa and Hildegard were in their migraines) but rather a wonderful similarity in the anguish and inspiration expressed. Zulawski, like a mystic, presents removal from an identifiable world (be it the dissolution of a marriage or exile from a country) as a trauma that changes the form of places. The film unfolds as an exploration of that shifting terrain, awesome revelations borne from the struggles of a new identity. *Possession* is not a soothing film, nor is it really horrifying. Instead it is a work that offers consolation on the topic of not knowing one's place.

Works Cited

Bird, Daniel, and Stephen Thrower. "Cinema Superactivity: An Interview with Andrzej Zulawski." In *Possession*. Mondo Vision, 2014. 33–54.

Flusser, Vilém. "The Challenge of the Migrant." In *The Freedom of the Migrant*. Tr. Kenneth Kronenberg. Urbana: University of Illinois Press, 2003. 1–20.

Gallagher, Daniel. "Two Main Works on Light and Darkness." Received by Nathan Chazan, 20 November 2017.

Heidegger, Martin. "Building Dwelling Thinking." In *Basic Writings*. Ed. David Farrell Krell. New York: Harper Perennial Modern Thought, 2008. 347–63.

Hildegard of Bingen. *Selections from Her Writings*. Tr. Mother Columbia Hart and Jane Bishop. Foreword by Homer Hickham. San Francisco: HarperSanFrancisco, 2005.

Hildegard of Bingen. *The Personal Correspondence of Hildegard of Bingen*. Tr. Joseph L. Baird. Oxford: Oxford University Press, 2005.

Hildegard of Bingen. "Epistolarium." In *Latin 3204—Lectiones,* ed. Daniel Gallagher. Ithaca, NY: Cornell University, 2017. 103–4.

Jazowska, Marta. "Andrjez Zulawski." *Culture.Pl*, culture.pl/en/artist/andrzej-zulawski. Accessed 5 December 2017.

Lugo, Alex. Personal interview. 21 September 2017.

St. Teresa of Avila. *The Collected Works of St. Teresa of Avila Volume 2*. Tr. Kieran Kavanaugh and Otilio Rodriguez. Washington, DC: ICS Publications, 1980.

Tarkovsky, Andrei. *Time Within Time: The Diaries, 1970–1986*. London: Faber & Faber, 1994.

Varene, Carine. "Possession, Andrzej Zulawski." In *Possession*. Mondo Vision, 2014. 70–72.

Zulawski, Andrzej, director. *On The Silver Globe*. Zespól Filmowy "Kadr," 1988.

Zulawski, Andrzej, director. *Possession*. Gaumont, 1981.

Full House

Hank Wagner

DARRELL SCHWEITZER. *The Dragon House*. Rockville, MD: Wildside Press, April 2018. 166 pp. $12.99 tpb. ISBN: 9781479438211.

As *The Dragon House* begins, thirteen-year-old Edward Longstretch is riding in the family car with his parents, and his older sister, Margaret, traveling to their new home in the wilds of northeastern Pennsylvania. The home proves to be more of a castle than a mere house, huge, "with more gables and turrets and high windows and strange turnings of the roof than the eye could take in at once." Edward, who feels a strange kinship with the house, soon learns he has the ability to travel through its very walls and floors, catching glimpses of strange environs, and unexpected inhabitants, as he explores its mysteries. Doing so, he comes to appreciate his true heritage and his heretofore unknown destiny, learning he is a key player in a cosmic drama where the fate of the world, and, indeed, the universe, hangs in the balance. He gamely accepts his strange, burdensome birthright, bravely plunging ahead into a conflict against extremely daunting, supremely evil opponents, whose only goals are chaos and destruction.

Weighing in at a mere 166 pages, *The Dragon House* certainly has the feel of a fat fantasy novel, if not the heft. Rich in story, incident, and character, almost totally lacking in exposition, it hurtles by at a dizzying pace, as Schweitzer breathlessly but concisely spins his tale of dragons, magic, and universal conflict, even as he nods at the absurdity and audacity of it all in numerous knowing asides and allusions. In so doing, he touches on numerous tropes and topics, delivering a fantasy bildungsroman that would give John Clute a migraine, should he attempt to categorize it. An entry in the renowned *Encyclopedia of Fantasy* would feature a plethora of headings/citations including, but not limited to:

Horror; Fantasy; Perception; Parody; Homage; Joseph Campbell; Hero; Hero's Journey; Dragons; Mentors; Magic; Magical Houses; Mystery; Haunted Houses; Spirits; Villains; Good and Evil; Cosmic Evil; Cosmic Conflict; Mystical Tomes; Sorcery; Avatars; Wizards; Talismans; Reality; Alien Races; Mash-up; Bellairs; Rowling; and many, many more, which I am no doubt omitting.

Light, breezy and whimsical, yet erudite, and displaying a keen, broad sense of humor and deep self-consciousness and self-awareness, *The Dragon House* represents a significant departure from Schweitzer's previous novel length work in the dark fantasy and horror genres. But, in the final analysis, it proves to be a welcome, if slight, diversion for readers, regardless of age.

Ringing in Apocalypse

Christopher Ropes

DAVID PEAK. *Corpsepaint*. Petaluma, CA: Word Horde, 2018. 240 pp. $15.95 tpb. ISBN: 978-1-939905-38-3.

Black Metal fans are very often looking for the "darkest, most evil thing" ever. Many of these fans are lost in the past—the days of Mayhem, Burzum, and Les Légions Noire. Those standard bearers for darkness and evil. The early '90s Second Wave of Black Metal—pulsing and oozing out of Europe like a cancerous growth.

Whether readers of David Peak's masterful *Corpsepaint* are among these foul hordes or are only aware of Black Metal as a hellish rumor of criminal activity and twisted youth, they will find much to love in the book. Those with limited or nonexistent experience with Black Metal may even find themselves intrigued enough after reading it to check out some YouTube videos—I would recommend Mayhem's *De Mysteriis Dom Sathanas*—to see if the music lives up to the aura of hellishness Peak depicts in his book.

Personally, I don't run around in corpsepaint, I've never burned a church, but the music soothes my inner demons by feeding them on Art, rather than on destructive impulses. That is, in large part, what I love about the music. Thomas Ligotti wrote in the introduction to one of his books, and I paraphrase, that the consolation of horror is finding out that someone else has the same nightmares. That is the appeal of Black Metal to me. Someone else holds the same demons in their heart.

Briefly, the book centers around Max, an aspiring Black Metal musician, and Roland, a drummer for hire working with Max to create an album that will blow away Max's early output. Max is a clear reflection, or characterization, of some American Black Metal musicians, such as Blake Judd of Nachmystium—a drug abuser; a people abuser; a legendary figure whose talent for getting himself into trouble with fans and fellow musicians outstrips any musical talent he may have. Max's band, Angelus Mortis, suffers the fate of many Black Metal bands. When someone brings up their work, they are usually referring to the band's first few albums, a phenomenon so pervasive in extreme music circles that there are memes mocking it.

Roland and Max are the recipients of an all-expenses-paid trip to the Ukraine to record at the infamous compound of Wisdom of Silenus, a far-right Ukrainian band rumored to have killed one of its own members for not being "true" enough. This resonates with real-life rumors of bands in NSBM (National Socialist Black Metal) circles killing their own for insufficient commitment to the cause of racial purity. One such case is the Russian circle of bands known as Blazebirth Hall, who allegedly killed a member for those reasons.

Despite the violence often associated with Black Metal, be it real or a rumor turned legend, *Corpsepaint* peels away the metaphysical layers of the entire Black Metal worldview and creates a sense of cosmic malevolence and potent evil that is usually only hinted at in the musical projects associated with the genre. By the time Max and Roland are in the Ukraine, things are too far gone and far too late for them and for the reader. Every character, major and minor, is drawn by a voracious hunger from the outer darkness into a series of violent and depraved acts that can truly only have one culmination. As such, the utterly bleak finale is completely earned.

Throughout, skillful use of foreshadowing builds a sense of foreboding that makes that ending perfect for what came before. The characterizations are sharp and cleverly utilize real Black Metal types to further inundate the novel with the sense of legitimacy. Max and Roland's apathetic nihilism is contrasted with the ferocious purity of the members of Wisdom of Silenus, adepts of the dark arts, communing with nature and obsessed with race and spirituality.

The difference between Max and Roland's diffidence and Wisdom of Silenus' rabid dedication to Evil illustrate Yeats's observation that "The best lack all conviction while the worst are full of passionate intensity." Our protagonists are not heroes by any stretch of the imagination, but compared to Wisdom of Silenus and the forces that the latter truck with, they are simply pawns of forces dedicated to destruction and annihilation beyond their merely human imaginings.

Corpsepaint is effortlessly epic, darker than a sensory deprivation tank, filled with the unbearable anger and sorrow that are at the heart of all evil and, thus, the very soul of Black Metal. Personally, I'm a huge fan of the musical genre, and I know that this novel is the book I had been awaiting for years—a piece of fiction that captures precisely that ineffable *something* which makes the music so effective. I'm not sure how relatable it would be to someone completely unfamiliar with the music, but the cosmic nature of the horrors, the beyond-Ligotti malignant bleakness, and the deviant goings-on would be sure to hook most avid horror fans. If you're not familiar with Black Metal when you start the book, you'll have glimpsed its dark soul by the time you finish it. I give this book my fervent recommendation.

Reflections on ICFA 39

J. T. Glover

Most people think of theme parks and mouse ears when it comes to fantasy in Orlando, but they haven't been to ICFA. The International Conference on the Fantastic in the Arts, which will see its fortieth anniversary in 2019, celebrates the fantastic in all media. From *Flash Gordon* to *Blade Runner 2049,* Hope Mirrlees to Saki, *Final Fantasy* to Henry Fuseli, Nnedi Okorafor to Caitlín R. Kiernan, all the different flavors of fantasy can be found there. Neither a standard academic conference nor a fan convention, its attendees include academics, artists, authors, editors, fans, independent scholars, publishers, and much more. Enough students, new academics, and new writers attend to suggest a bright future, and they come from around the world (to name a few from 2018: Austria, Canada, Finland, New Zealand, and Portugal). As ICFA happens in March, the weather hovers in the 70s by day, making for a pleasant holiday for those of us hailing from cooler climates, whether discussing new books over a drink in the cabana or lounging by the pool after sessions.

This year was my third ICFA, and as a writer, librarian, and scholar, I've never yet run out of things to do. This time I saw plenty of engaging, thought-provoking readings and panels, and I think *Dead Reckonings* readers would have found much to enjoy in those on early twentieth-century literary horror (Blackwood, Endore, de la Mare), on Robert E. Howard, and in the many panels connected with *Frankenstein*. This year's ICFA was one of many international events celebrating the famed novel's bicentennial—and dismemberment, artificial life, and grave robbing were a constant.

ICFA features multiple tracks of panels, often themed according to different divisions (Horror Literature, Film and Television, etc.), with an ongoing block of readings, so you can attend whatever moves you. There are delightful all-conference meals, including the culminating awards banquet, where the Crawford and other awards are given, and many opportunities for coffee or drinks with guests and attendees. Both the silent auction and the book room—a beloved Aladdin's Cave once stewarded by the late great David Hartwell—are not to be missed! From the most recent of horror and fantasy to hard-to-find Necronomicon Press publications, there's something for everyone.

My own activities at ICFA tend to constellate around horror, particularly Lovecraft. I had the pleasure of sitting on a panel discussion focused on *Weird Tales* and the evolution of weird fiction generally, along with Nike Sulway (2018's Guest of Honor), Tracy Stone, Jeffrey Shanks, and Sean Moreland (our moderator). The room was packed at an hour so early that many attendees were heretofore unaware of its existence, and we took the attendees down the weird path, from Le Fanu to Llewellyn, Wright to VanderMeer, Derleth to Bartlett.

Later I presented a paper ("Lies, Damned Lies, and Eldritch Statistics: Toward a Quantitative Analysis of Lovecraft's Literary Reputation") on a panel with Daniel Look and Tracy Stone entitled "The Ubiquitous Mr. Lovecraft." I've attended at least one Lovecraft or Lovecraft-related panel every time I've gone to ICFA, typically featuring vigorous and sometimes contentious discussion following, and this year was no different. I walked away from the panel with good questions to help guide my own next steps, and new friends for the journey . . . and the same can be said for the conference overall.

By the end of any such gathering, I'm typically ready for books and solitude, which made it all the more remarkable how much I enjoyed participating in the annual "Words & Worlds" prose reading, a long-running series where attending scholars who write fiction present their work. There, as in every session or reading I attended, I felt a sense of shared interest among us all, and that, together with ICFA's easygoing atmosphere, keeps me coming back to Florida in the spring, for those thought-provoking interactions with lovely people about strange and terrible things.

Ramsey's Rant: A Modicum of Blood

Ramsey Campbell

". . . a modicum of blood, shed with deliberation and carefully husbanded . . ."

So wrote M. R. James in 1929, in his essay "Some Remarks on Ghost Stories." He was listing elements he thought necessary to the ghost story (concerning which he would later write "Must there be horror? you ask. Yes, I think so."). Another, consistent with the first dictum I quote here, was reticence. To some extent he cited this as a reaction to the *Not at Night* anthologies, which he deplored ("I, *moi qui vous parle,* could undertake to make a reader physically sick, if I chose to think and write in terms of the Grand Guignol"). More than this, his fiction frequently exemplifies the principles he stated, and demonstrates how effective a touch of gruesomeness rather than excess of it can be. I'd argue that it makes the reader apprehensive that further horrors lie in wait, just as James is a master of the detail that shows just enough to suggest far worse. Consider the ghastly fate of Anders Bjornsen, given in less than a sentence, in "Count Magnus," or that of Paxton, equally succinctly conveyed, in "A Warning to the Curious." For this reader no more is necessary to imbue the entire tale with terror.

It often seems that just a solitary image is enough to take up residence in the shadows of the reader's mind. I suspect that those who know James can recognise any number of tales from less than a single sentence. Elsewhere, who can forget the mushy finger in "The Yellow Sign," or the grisly icicle in "A Visitor from Down Under," or Frank's deadly chant in "There's a Long, Long Trail A-Winding" (the nearest Russell Kirk ever comes to depicting violence, as far as I recall), or the condition of the unnamed corpse in "The Willows"? That said, some writers are impatient with restraint, and when their eagerness can produce work of the calibre of Clive Barker's early tales, say, or Joe Lansdale's *The Nightrunners,* it's admirably fruitful. The two tendencies have been in opposition at least since the Gothic novel (one extreme of which is surely the work of de Sade), and can sometimes be represented within the output of a single author. Despite or even possibly because it's so often suggested that extreme horror desensitises its audience, the subtler kind keeps returning too: it's splendidly represented these days in the work of various contemporary writers—Nina Allan, Reggie Oliver, Lynda E. Rucker, Michelle Paver, and Alison Moore, for just a few examples—and here's my hope that T. E. D. Klein soon breaks his literary silence.

Still, I suppose the accusation about the deadening of sensibilities is more often levelled at the cinema, which prompts me to say it's untrue in my case. I find that a flare of ferocity in a vintage film still conveys shock, precisely because of the period when it was made. Just this week I was startled by *The Covered Wagon,* almost a century old, in which the hero comes very close to gouging out the eyes of his adversary, having been incited by his best friend on the trek. Admittedly this was well before the advent of the Hays Code, but I'm prompted to ponder films that sprinkle the narrative with a small amount of gore or violence, all the more effective for the surrounding reticence. I believe they provide an experience akin to that offered by the tales I've cited.

The earliest that comes to mind is *Behind the Door* from 1919, in which Wallace Beery's villain suffers an atrocious fate, signified only by the intertitles and the reactions of those who find the corpse. The gang rape of the heroine is depicted just by implication, but startling all the same. A contemporary review in the *Exhibitors Herald* describes the villain's end as a just punishment. The recent Flicker Alley Blu-ray includes a Soviet release that substantially alters plot, character and politics. By my definition the finale of either version turns the film into horror.

Where do we find the first visually shocking images? Buñuel's first three films are spectacularly special cases, as is the unsimulated bloodletting in Dreyer's *Joan of Arc.* I submit as the earliest in commercial film (apart from the severed hands on the wire in *All Quiet on the Western Front*) Lugosi's treatment of the venereally infected woman in *Murders in the Rue Morgue,* a startlingly confrontational scene even for 1932, and the sewn lips that announce mutely how we're at the gleeful mercy of *Murders in the Zoo* (1933). Robert Bloch cited King Kong's careless way with the wrong woman in New York as a quintessential moment of horror, and the restored uncensored version contains several. The arena scenes in *Sign of the Cross* (1934)—eight minutes of virtually unrelieved sadism—hardly count as a moment of horror, but helped lend power to the Hays Code, previously flouted. Perhaps that year's *The Black Cat* represents horror's gesture of defiance before the genre had to rein itself back on the screen for a while. Certainly the flaying scene, though brief and shown only in silhouette, goes further than *Behind the Door* in terms of explicitness, and a year later *The Werewolf of London* confronts us with a face clawed by a lycanthrope, on the poster too.

After that Hollywood grows reticent for several years. Across the Atlantic Lugosi made *The Dark Eyes of London,* in which his evil doctor deafens a blind man, but this is an uncommon moment of sadism for the period (though perhaps also evidence that the British censor could be less strict with home-grown films). The effects of pushing a man's head through a radium tube in Schoedsack's *Dr. Cyclops* (1940) fade to black too swiftly to convey horror, although the late Eddie Jones maintained he'd originally seen a more explicit version in an English cinema. The surprise—given Val Lewton's justified reputation for reticence—is that Lewton revived gore in Hollywood horror.

The Leopard Man (1943) is famous for its modicum of blood, which trickles over a transom to signify savagery beyond—a suggestive alternative to the gruesomeness of Cornell Woolrich's source novel. By contrast, the final fight in *The Ghost Ship* (1943) is shockingly savage and painfully graphic— at least as much so as any of its contemporaries in crime. That genre saw a gradual escalation of violence too, from the fallen Sam Spade being kicked in the head in *The Maltese Falcon* (1941) to the agonising torture of Dennis O'Keefe's T-Man in Anthony Mann's 1947 film (and I'd argue that Raymond Burr's way with a flambé dish in Mann's *Raw Deal,* made a year later, leads to the coffee pot in *The Big Heat* and the Coke bottle in *The Long Goodbye,* not to mention the pure gratuitousness of the glassing of Sid James in *No Orchids for Miss Blandish*). Such scenes in film noir perform a function similar to that of the gore shot in horror—representing an omnipresent threat of violence. Graphic moments may be found in a few more wartime horror films—the explicit dissolution sunlight brings to *The Return of the Vampire,* though not the censored British release, and *The Picture of Dorian Gray* (the Albright portrait, blazing into colour). The pretty thoroughly insipid *She-Wolf of London* (1946) surely marks the low point of withheld horror and of the Universal monster cycle, despite the false promises of the poster ("Wild weird shuddery thrills! Half woman—half monster . . . Night-creeping horror blazing a trail of blood!"). It was time for at least a hint of the explicit to return, and the fifties make such moments something of a staple of horror cinema.

Did Britain seize the baton? Certainly *The Quatermass Xperiment* (1955) contains two grisly glimpses, all the more effective for their terseness, and the following year *X the Unknown* (conceived as a sequel to the previous film, a proposition vetoed by Nigel Kneale) retains the brevity but intensifies the grue. 1957 sees a gorily rent throat in *Cat Girl,* a curious amalgam of themes from Val Lewton and Monogram, raised to a considerably higher level by Barbara Shelley's performance. The shot is missing from some prints, as is a giant insect chewing a soldier's face in the same year's *Strange World of Planet X*. Neither shot survived in the original British releases, which were cut to avoid an X certificate (as was *The Incredible Shrinking Man,* where the spider ended up dead but not bled). Some shocks passed into legend because they were missing from most copies of a film: the cow blinding an alien invader in the otherwise comedic *Invasion of the Saucer Men*, the rat-squeezing scene in *The Hideous Sun Demon*. By contrast, the closeups of the drooling giant insect in *The Black Scorpion* were celebrated on the British poster, which proclaimed "Uncut! Shown *exactly* as filmed!" Indeed it was, perhaps to the surprise of the distributor.

The gore shot or shock image was crucial to the films of

Dead Reckonings

William Castle—the gruesome corpse in the opened coffin of *Macabre,* the severed head in a suitcase from *The House on Haunted Hill,* the startling decapitation (disliked by the screenwriter, Robert Bloch) in *Straitjacket.* At the time they felt like threats that the film might go further (in the case of *Macabre,* coupled with insuring viewers against death by fright). Roger Corman spiced his overall restraint with stabs of relatively explicit grue—a sanguinary trickle in *The Wasp Woman* and *Not of This Earth,* a mutilation in *Attack of the Crab Monsters.* Since the special effects tend to be shaky, perhaps these details add to the overall seriousness of the films— there's certainly no sense of spoof. A minor monster film like *The Monster of Piedras Blancas* is enlivened by the sight of a pair of severed heads, though not on its British release. Occasionally family films were invaded by horror: an explicit dissolution in *The Time Machine* (though not in the British print), the charred men in *St. George and the Seven Curses* (which was rated X in Britain, ridding it of its intended audience). There's no refuge.

When did grisliness begin to spread throughout narratives? Contemporary hostile reviews might suggest it was when Hammer Films found colour, but even those productions were sparing in their gruesomeness. I believe the change was signalled by Mario Bava. *Caltiki* heralds his later explicitness— the uncommonly slimy skeleton of a victim does—but it's *La Maschera del Demonio* that marries violence and lyricism, beauty and horror. Its visuals combine the atmospheric qualities that Universal developed in their monochrome monster films with imaginative shocks—the application of the titular mask, and especially the swarm of insects consequent upon its removal.

Overall restraint barbed with infrequent horror is seldom to be found in films these days. There are splendid exceptions. *The Borderlands* (retitled as *Final Prayer*) powerfully and claustrophobically delivers by saving its uncanny violence until the very end. *The VVitch* and *Hereditary* husband their horrors to concentrate on mounting insidious dread. Is this a growing trend? I hope so, but I'll support anything that enriches the imagination. That's what we're about, or should be.

What Is Anything
When Considered Twice?

S. T. JOSHI. *What Is Anything? Memoirs of a Life in Lovecraft.*
New York: Hippocampus Press, 2018. 350 pp. $45.00 hc. Limited edition of 250 copies. ISBN 978-1-61498-220-3.

This issue of *Dead Reckonings* may find readers wondering if they are seeing double as it features two reviews of S. T. Joshi's memoir, *What Is Anything? Memoirs of a Life in Lovecraft,* on top of two pieces by Joshi and two reviews of two separate works by Josh Malerman. While two articles by Joshi is nothing new to the pages of *Dead Reckonings*—and always welcome—and two reviews of two different books by the same author can be justified—particularly given the different assessments reached by our reviewers—the choice to review the same book twice may strike readers as . . . odd?

The reason for this is that each review offers a unique perspective. In Donald Sidney-Fryer's piece there is an interspersing of his personal relationship with Joshi throughout the years—a knowledge that transcends the memoir. In contrast, Géza Reilly looks to the memoir as an invitation and opportunity to learn more about the figure who has so influenced and informed his own understanding of Lovecraft and weird fiction. The pieces complement each other, and it is hoped that readers will come away with a deeper appreciation for S. T. Joshi and his memoir reading both.—ED.

Existential Remembrance

Donald Sidney-Fryer

Although he has written a sizeable amount of fiction (short stories and novels), and has had it published (and generally well received), S. T. Joshi has made his mark—and a quite considerable one—primarily as a literary critic and editor involving not only the works of H. P. Lovecraft but just as much the fictional output of Ambrose Bierce, Algernon Blackwood, Ramsey Campbell, Lord Dunsany, William Hope Hodgson, M. R. James, Thomas Ligotti, and Gore Vidal, not to leave out the complete poetry (and poetic dramas) of George Sterling and Clark Ashton Smith (three volumes' worth for each poet, and in Smith's case also including his poetic translations), as well as full-scale bibliographies for several writers enumerated here. No less than any monk in some medieval scriptorium, Joshi has functioned as a dedicated copyist but with typewriter and computer, and as rigorously as any redactor with pen and parchment in some remote monastery. David E. Schultz as his typesetting collaborator (creating books, qua books, for Hippocampus Press) has materially and masterfully aided and abetted Joshi at virtually every step, and patently deserves emphatic acknowledgment.

As an addendum to much demanding labors, Joshi's autobiography reflects great honor on the autobiographer, no less than Derrick Hussey as the publisher. It is a handsome hardcover volume, 6 × 9 × 1 inches, totaling 346 pp., 38 lines per page for the main text, pp. 10–322; the index, double-columned, occupies pp. 323–46. Photographic illustrations (one page each, on both sides) appear between pp. 46–47, 156–57, 262–63, putting on view diverse friends, family, and colleagues. A disarming photo of Joshi at age four (while holding a toy vehicle in both hands), taken at Poona, India, features as the frontispiece. Yes, he is indeed a winsome little guy.

In *What Is Anything?* Joshi discloses the truly staggering achievement of his life and career up to his sixtieth birthday, celebrated with friends in Manhattan on Friday evening, 22 June 2018. In honor of that event, Derrick Hussey (owner-editor of Hippocampus Press) has issued Joshi's autobiography. Overall it makes for a fascinating read, no less than a deeply revelatory one. (Among other aspects he reveals a very nice sense of humor, and a sly sense of wit.) As it befits a critic-editor who has perforce read, re-read, copied, and critically edited the works of Bierce, Blackwood, Lovecraft, Sterling, and Smith, amid many others—all of whom are master prosateurs as well—Joshi commands a ready and supple style, at once suave, attractive, and very well informed, and in fact erudite.

Merely acknowledging the depth, scope, and massiveness of Joshi's overall accomplishment seems at least an understatement. All people seriously interested in modern imaginative literature remain seriously in Joshi's debt on behalf of all the writers on whose output he has done significant labor, including impeccably corrected and correlated texts. Correcting texts, comparing the printed and received ones against the original versions in holograph and in typed form, represents a tremendous challenge as well as an onerous task, which no one inexperienced in such activity should ever underestimate. Among his other skills and abilities Joshi possesses a lively, well-developed, and well-informed love and appreciation of poetry whether traditional or non-traditional, a capacity by no means common to American Anglophones. A miracle!

This book has laid to rest many misconceptions that I, with others, have incorrectly entertained. First, although Derrick Hussey and Joshi have had a partnership with each other from the very start of Hippocampus Press (1999), it has turned out be to more of a creative collaboration. It is not a business partnership. The biggest revelation for this reviewer—apart from the depth, breadth, and sheer quality of Joshi's literary work (especially on behalf of Lovecraft as well as many other writers)—Joshi is truly a man of letters!—is learning of Joshi as a bona fide musician: composer, choral singer, and violinist, particularly the last. This places him thus, not in the clan of Vieuxtemps or Paganini, but in the same class as the ballet-music composers and conductors of the 1800s, not less than that of the violinists for the ballet rehearsals, the répétiteurs, or "repetitors" (the same word but translated back from Russian).

As this reviewer followed the text faithfully from page one through 346, he discovered that he has many affinities with Joshi—Joshi has assembled and edited a new Clark Ashton Smith bibliography, to be published evidently during 2018. When sojourning in Paris, Joshi has avoided visiting the Louvre—it would have resulted in an exhausting and never-ending experience! I have also avoided the museum for the same reason (although I have crossed through the main or outer courtyard with the sizeable glass pyramid many times), even though I have visited Paris at least half a dozen times. One of the more pleasant aspects of Joshi's writing style is his apt and extensive love of language, and in particular his refreshing use of *piquant* throughout the autobiography. *Piquant*, indeed!

Joshi is remarkably consistent in his opinions and preferences. He has always emphasized that, in his opinion, Clark Ashton Smith ranks higher as a poet (no less than as a practitioner of the poem in prose) than as a fictioneer. I beg to disagree. I hold with Smith himself that his best fiction occupies an equally high place with his poetry. However, when by the time he came to edit and publish a collection of Smith's best prose and poetry through Penguin Classics, Joshi had adopted a more appreciative critical stance. This collection appeared in 2014 as *The Dark Eidolon and Other Fantasies*. It marked an important step in Smith's being recognized and promoted as a "canonical" author.

For the most part, I agree with Joshi's take on many classic authors and classic texts, at least by the modern weird masters, say, of the last two centuries, that is, since the late 1700s or early 1800s. And yes, Machen's last novel *The Green Round* is disappointing, or in Joshi's own phrase, "a pretty sorry piece of work." The publication of some fiction by Machen in the U.S. by Arkham House would have been better served by continuing Machen's two last collections of understated stories *The Cosy Room* and *The Children of the Pool*.

In the Epilogue, Joshi presents a list of possible (monumental) projects that he might like to do, now that he has completed the full program of hard labor on behalf of H. P. Lovecraft and his *oeuvre,* but he has doubts as to whether he has the energy to follow up on any of them now that he is sixty. After all that he has done on Lovecraft's behalf, how much more could anyone accomplish, that is, apart from certain specialized areas of research and examination? Joshi has achieved all the labor needed, the basic, the further, and the extraneous. And he has done it all exemplarily well, never mind all the other authors who have benefitted from his efforts, from Bierce and Machen to Ramsey Campbell and Thomas Ligotti.

In my own examination of Joshi as a dynamic creative force in modern imaginative literature (whether fantasy, science fiction, or science fantasy), I find much that amazes and astonishes me. I am not prone to criticize him and his labor in any way. However, I would like to express one regret, but only after the following discussion. Joshi wrote a negative review of Peter Ruber's anthology of short stories *Arkham's Masters of Horror* (2000)—a negative response that seems to have been justified. Consequently Joshi "was declared *persona non grata* by April Derleth, August Derleth's daughter, [then] the chief owner" of Arkham House. Much later, Joshi "had actually re-established contract with April Derleth, who did not hold it against me that I still regarded her father's efforts on Love-craft's work and reputation as more harmful than helpful." I profoundly disagree.

Given the radically different period in which August Der-leth lived, and when he first began promulgating Lovecraft and his *oeuvre* with the first published omnibus volume of Lovecraft's collected fiction (during the late 1930s and early 1940s) among other creative writings such as his essays and poetry)—and given the circumstances of how Derleth had to make his living as a professional writer and editor during the 1930s through the 1940s, 1950s, and 1960s—I honestly don't see how he could have done any better than what he did. It is easy to criticize anyone in retrospect, long after the fact, but Derleth had much else to do besides promoting Lovecraft, even with the assistance of Donald Wandrei and others, even if a primary goal.

Without the pioneering work on and for Lovecraft that Derleth achieved, just how much better would Joshi himself have fared, not only following Derleth but even correcting him, as it then seemed necessary and justified. I do not argue that Joshi did not do something right following Derleth—he did, and then something more! Derleth's work in a sense pre-pared the way for Joshi and what he has achieved in his own turn, including the mistakes committed by Derleth as he was living his life to the fullest, and earning his living by a prodi-gious amount of creative writing, whether for books or peri-odicals. At this late date I would like to suggest a somewhat more evenhanded approach and evaluation, such as John Hae-fele has recently attempted in *A Look Behind the Derleth Mythos*

(2012; rev. ed. 2014). As Don Herron has averred, Derleth in his own manner was a titan in the field of modern imaginative literature, giving book publication to many meritorious authors who probably could not have found it before Tolkien and the renaissance of fantasy that followed him.

I am not exculpating Derleth's errors, but merely wish to suggest that, without his initial promotion or promulgation of Lovecraft, nothing might have happened on the scale that it eventually did until much later. I don't think highly in general of the Cthulhu Mythos per se (it is but a strategic part of the apparatus making up much of Lovecraft's fiction, especially the later and longer tales), nor do I think highly of the Cthulhu Mythos tales written by others in imitation of Lovecraft's own, above all Derleth's curiously inept attempts as embodied in *The Mask of Cthulhu* and *The Trail of Cthulhu*.

I had aided Derleth off and on with little bits and pieces of editorial work (including the preparation of several manuscripts of material in uncollected book-form by Ashton Smith). At Derleth's request (as part of our literary apprentice work) I took on the task of typing the manuscript for *The Trail of Cthulhu*, but as I got into the typing I found the stories to be so formulaic, and the style so indifferent and so unsavory, that I gave up the task and returned the material (probably tearsheets from some pulp magazines) to Derleth. He accepted my defection with good grace and good humor. (The excuse that I gave for my non-performance, insofar as I can recall, may have been the pressure from our university studies.) I believe that someone else accepted and executed the task.

In regard to the thorny question or issue of the Cthulhu Mythos imitations, I make one exception, and moreover by Derleth himself: *The Lurker at the Threshold,* a rare success as Fritz Leiber agreed. May Joshi fare better with his own critics than Derleth has!

What Is Anything?—both the title and the question—is an existential conundrum.

All He Cared to Tell

Géza A. G. Reilly

Reading *What Is Anything?* makes me feel as though I've wasted my life. Not in a brute or unkind way, but one cannot help but compare one's achievements to S. T. Joshi's when reading his memoir. Far be it from me to cast aspersions, but I would imagine that almost all readers would find themselves asking "where does he find the *time*?" at some point or other over the course of the book's 322-page length and suspect that a deal with the devil has occurred. *What Is Anything?* is indeed a remarkable catalog of Joshi's life and career. However, it leans far more toward the latter than the former.

It should be noted that a memoir is distinct from an autobiography, of course, and as such it is not uncommon at all for a work of this sort to focus more on one's career than one's personal life. Still and all, I would imagine that anyone who is drawn to read *What Is Anything?* does not need to be told all *that* much about Joshi's work. The book will likely be valuable as a historical artifact, and that fact alone possibly redeems its inclusion on our shelves. Still, I am ultimately uncertain as to how much I got out of the book. Despite its small print run of 250 copies, *What Is Anything?* received fine treatment from Hippocampus Press. It is an attractive volume, written in Joshi's regular clear prose, and it bears an excellent cover illustration by his longtime collaborator Jason C. Eckhardt.

The fact of the matter is that Joshi seems to be the sort of person whose life *is* their work, and thus that aspect of his time on this Earth overshadows almost every other part of his past. Perhaps this is unfair, because we do learn a not insignificant amount about Joshi's life from his birth in 1958 to close to his sixtieth birthday in 2018. Most repeated are the insights we are given on his various personal touchstones: Joshi's love of music, his charming care for cats, his various personal relationships, his experiences as a world traveler, and his family's history all show up between discussions of his work. Still, these are brief flashes rather than the meat of the affair.

Paradoxically, Joshi does seem to *over*share at least once. In the preface, Joshi says that "my innate reticence and reserve [. . .] render me incapable of speaking of intimate personal matters, especially since many other individuals with whom my life has been entwined over the years are still alive, and I do not care to invade their privacy or my own." Fair enough! However, late in *What Is Anything?* Joshi calls out a former friend by name in a gauche listing of that person's purported affronts, which seems to fly in the face of his previous assertion and leaves a bad taste in the reader's mouth. This conflict between over- and under-sharing makes the end of the memoir less satisfying than it could be, though it must be said that Joshi's occasional statements of decorum are on their own perfectly palatable (such as when he states "It is not to my purpose in this memoir to go into intimate details of my private life" in reference to a romantic partner).

Perhaps due to its prevalence, *What Is Anything?* is strongest when discussing Joshi's intimate involvement in the weird, atheist, and liberal literary communities. This is not to say that Joshi's descriptions of his attitudes or efforts are always agreeable, of course. His exuberance toward what he has termed "satirical criticism" (which, perhaps with tongue in cheek, he claims is "a whole new subgenre of literature") tends to gloss over some valid complaints about his reviewing style, for example. Equally, I was rather shocked by some of his complaints about theory-based approaches to the study and critique of literature and standard journal practices (including peer review). Whether or not Joshi realizes that others might validly consider these things flaws in his approach to his work, I cannot say, but I suspect he would not care.

I do not personally know S. T. Joshi, though, for the sake of honesty, I have exchanged pleasant correspondence with him here and there. For the most part, and like most of us, I know the man only through his work—the vast majority of which is excellent and worthy of reference. When I began reading *What Is Anything?* I had the hope that I would come to know Joshi a bit more than I had before. Well, that is what I got: I know Joshi a *bit* better now, but not enough to be fully satisfied in light of the potential of the project. Although I do recommend *What Is Anything?* on the basis of its shockingly well-remembered history of Joshi and various literary communities, I fear I can really only recommend it on that note alone.

There is an idea in the critical theory scholarship of English literature that language is a process of mediation. That is, when we read we are never experiencing anything directly other than the act of reading. We are always sitting at a distance of at least one remove from whatever the subject of the text might be (as we are from anything that we need to describe to ourselves in language). I had hoped that *What Is Anything?* might bring me closer to understanding S. T. Joshi in one way or another, but what I have been given only reminds me of the distance between us. Instead of getting to know Joshi, *What Is Anything?* allows the reader really to know only Joshi's *career*. I wished to find a fellow traveler in its pages, but what I found was a set of accomplishments. However well written the text is—and it is, again, quite well written—that, ultimately, cannot possibly be satisfying if it is all there is.

The Case for *Weird Tales* Replicas

Ryne Davis

Earlier this year, Girasol Collectibles of Ontario, Canada, went out of business. They were the only company ever to produce exact, page-for-page replicas of the now infamous *Weird Tales*. Girasol begun its operation by reprinting the first four years of *Weird Tales,* 1923 to 1927, in full; a welcome beginning as it made available, and affordable, some of the rarest and most price-prohibitive issues of the pulp. Eventually Girasol began reprinting issues from the "Golden Age" of *Weird Tales*, that is, the 1930s, with an emphasis on stories and serials that featured Robert E. Howard's most famous creation, Conan.

While one may be able to appreciate Girasol's efforts, the project on a whole begs a question: why do we need replicas of *Weird Tales* at all when most of the good stuff contained within them can be found in anthologies and other more convenient forms? I would argue that there is an undeniable historical importance in preserving what was once the primary source for the fiction of H. P. Lovecraft, Clark Ashton Smith, Robert E. Howard, and several other notable writers. However, I believe there is more to it than that. There's something about experiencing the whole package, flawed though it is, as readers first experienced it so many decades ago—from classic stories of its most beloved writers, to the often stunning artwork of Virgil Finlay and Margaret Brundage, to the readers' (and sometimes fellow contributors') reactions and opinions in "The Eyrie," the magazine's letters department. Even the silly ads for psychic readings and free spectacles have a certain charm to them.

That *Weird Tales* and other magazines of the era enjoy the reputation as "pulps" speaks to another reason for reprints. The pulps were so named because they were made with cheap wood-pulp paper and tended to fall apart very quickly. The high acid content in the paper caused it to turn yellow and become brittle. Original copies, even those kept in "excellent" condition, cannot help but reveal that they are aging rapidly. And yet, these original copies can sell for hundreds of dollars and more, despite the fact that they are disintegrating. Casual fans, and fans without money to burn, who want to experience the magazine in its original form are left in the dust. This is where a company like Girasol is so valuable: they made these magazines available to a wide audience, not just collectors.

There appears to be a strong demand for the old magazines in general. Not only are there several companies that reproduce classic titles, but there are large conventions dedicated to them, such as Windy City Pulp and Paper, a yearly event just outside Chicago. I attended last April, and while there was considerable space given to books and artwork, the focus was definitely on the vintage pulps—*Weird Tales* figuring most prominently. At this event, I purchased two of Girasol's replicas for a slightly marked-up price. I had noticed this happening elsewhere on the secondhand market as soon as Girasol closed its doors. In an ironic twist of fate, magazines that were made for people who couldn't, or didn't want to, pay collector's prices were now becoming collector's items themselves.

Sixty-five issues of *Weird Tales* were reproduced by Girasol Collectibles before the company went out of business. Since that magazine's first run from 1923 to 1954 totaled 279 issues, the majority of those have never been replicated and are rapidly deteriorating. With the seemingly perennial growth in popularity of H. P. Lovecraft, it is a shame that the publication indelibly linked to his name is virtually unavailable except at exorbitant prices. With so much legendary content originating in the pages of *Weird Tales,* I believe it deserves preservation and to be more widely available to fans of weird fiction. At least one company, Art's Books and Images, LLC, has seemingly picked up where Girasol left off, offering facsimiles of some issues of *Weird Tales* and other pulps at lulu.com/wyllie. It is to be hoped that this niche industry will continue to flower.

Transformative Visions

Acep Hale

PRIYA SHARMA, *All the Fabulous Beasts*. Pickering, ON: Undertow Publications. 2018. 287 pp. $25.00 tpb ISBN 978-1-988964-02-7.

Priya Sharma knows that nature is false; Nature, as a separate space to which one must travel, is a concept concocted by the Victorians and reinforced through intervening generations. We are nature and walk amongst it within our homes, cities, and places of employment. It is only because this idea of Nature allows us to retain our most cherished myth, humanity's fall from grace, in a post-Nietzschean world, that we cling so firmly to this artificial construct while creating new myth cycles to bolster the old. This knowledge allows Sharma to use her considerable mythopoetic skills to craft exquisite tales of transformation that horrify and enchant simultaneously.

Sharma has beyond all doubt mastered the short story. Before going any further let me say I will be surprised if a stronger collection arrives in 2018. As I completed each story, I found myself eager to pass the collection along to my partner so I could share and discuss the wonders within.

One of Sharma's many strengths lies in her considerable gift for characterization. Without succumbing to the oft-repeated demand for likable characters, she fashions complex personalities with whom readers may resonate. Sharma's creations are all too human. No matter how fantastic the story, this element ensnares the reader within Sharma's exquisitely woven prose as surely as the weight of family entangles her characters.

That said, *All the Fabulous Beasts* suffers the dangers of a magician's trick repeated. By the time I reached this volume's titular story, Sharma's formula for her tales' construction grew familiar.

This is a danger for any single-author collection. When the

stories are spread throughout anthology appearances or magazines, as all but two of them were, one would never notice such a thing; but when the stories are read one after the other the chances grow exponentially of readers noticing a writer's sleight-of-hand. Given that Sharma has been publishing her work for close to a decade, I believe she has a wider range than what is on display within *All the Fabulous Beasts*. This expanded range may have provided shade for Sharma's legerdemain, yet given this tight focus, one is allowed the ease of observation. I would not place the shortcomings of *All the Fabulous Beasts* with the writing yet rather in the editorial role.

There are sixteen tales in the book. Standouts include "A Son of the Sea," tackles both liminality and transformation within it's twenty-five pages as a young man returns to Hong Kong following his father's death, seeking knowledge of a mother he never knew. As "A Son of the Sea" aptly demonstrates, Sharma is an accomplished technician, yet Chekhov's gun is adhered to so stringently within this collection that by the time I reached "A Son of the Sea" I felt as if I were engrossed in a locked-room mystery while reading her character's musings, because I was distracted enough by the formula to know that morsels of seemingly inconsequential information would become part of a grand reveal.

The same can be said with the structuring of "A Son of the Sea." Open with an intriguing yet purposefully vague paragraph, jump backwards in time to fill in the personal mythology/history of the character, return momentarily to present time as the story's plot demands, repeat this cycle to the conclusion of the story. There is nothing wrong with this approach; it's simply when the method becomes habitual that it comes at the price of a story's vitality, no matter how transcendent the writing. Other ways to work with foreshadowing are well known, and perhaps should have been considered. As I wrote previously, if there were a space of time between readings, this structuring would not be so apparent. I feel editors working with writers on their collections should take special care so as to avoid this situation.

That said, there is a saying amongst magicians, "the trick is not the method and the method is not the trick." One watches films of Slydini performing simply to marvel at the grace, skill, and beauty with which he worked, all while in full knowledge of the way he adroitly manipulated the audience's attention. The exact same may be said of Sharma's writing, which is so thoroughly enchanting that even with the caveats above I found myself thoroughly captivated and engrossed by her effortless flow. On the few occasions when she veers from the paths blazed by Angela Carter and solidified by Rikki Ducornet, Sharma has the stunning ability to snap one's head back with panache. "The Show" is a devastating piece about a televised paranormal show gone awry that brings to mind the utterly effective *Ghostwatch* special the BBC aired two decades ago, while "Small Town Stories" recalls the work of Joel Lane without sacrificing any of the numerous gifts that make Sharma's works so compelling on their own. In similar form "The Ballad of Boomtown," a story that contains elements of deep time and scapegoating, brought to mind the ability of Pamela Zoline's ability to expand the quotidian.

Another story where all the elements fuse into a compelling and singularly eerie presence is "The Rising Tide," wherein a medical resident retires to a remote location in order to come to terms with a traumatic event. Here Sharma's intuitive understanding of Tim Morton's concept of a *dark ecology,* where the environment or Nature are not separate processes from humanity yet rather "ooze uncannily around us," melds seamlessly with her innate comprehension of the human condition and her medical background to bring us a tale that is truly unsettling.

I must confess I do not understand the choice of cover illustration used for the paperback. While it is indeed a beautiful piece, it looks as if it would be more appropriate gracing the front of a shōjo manga and does not tonally match the writing contained within. Sarah Ahhmed, a prominent scholar and theorist of Affect Theory, has written how "a feeling becomes an instrument or technique," and we must be appreciative of how these techniques are utilized to interpret what is happening around us, how affect is wielded to manipulate us. With a lesser publishing house I would have shrugged off this misstep; and yet, with a publishing house such as Undertow

Publications, one known to hold itself to a higher standard of aesthetics, this choice of cover and the inclusion of the clip-art snake skeleton at the beginning of each of the sixteen stories seem a misstep from one usually attuned to the effect that the physical presence the book itself has upon the reader.

That said, *All the Fabulous Beasts* is an incredibly strong collection from a fabulously adroit writer that should not be missed. Given the number of times I interrupted my wife's work to read her passages of Sharma's prose, I'm surprised we're not divorced or separated at the very least. With a broader range on offer, as "The Rising Tide" shows she can handle with chilling élan, I foresee Sharma's name on the lips of weird fiction fans the world over. I myself will eagerly snap up all her future works.

A Visionary Work Renew'd

Sam Gafford and The joey Zone

WILLIAM HOPE HODGSON. *The House on the Borderland*. Introduction by Alan Moore; illustrated by John Coulthart; afterword by Iain Sinclair. Dublin: Swan River Press, 2018. 216 pp. €30.00 unsigned hardcover; €40.00 signed hardcover; €50.00 signed hardcover with CD. ISBN 978-1-78380-021-6.

Gafford and Zone were participants in "William Hope Hodgson: An Appreciation," a panel held at NecronomiCon 2017 in Providence, R.I. Both are longtime admirers of Hodgson, but Gafford in particular has been one of the main authorities on the writer and his work in addition to founding *Sargasso: The Journal of William Hope Hodgson Studies*.

Swan River Press is an independent small-press publisher based in Dublin, dedicated to supernatural and fantastic literature. It is responsible for high-quality editions of authors such as Bram Stoker, Joseph Sheridan Le Fanu, and the journal *The Green Book*. The Swan River Press edition of *The House on the Borderland* is a noteworthy appearance of Hodgson's novel, not only in its deluxe presentation, complete with an introduction by Alan Moore, an afterword by Iain Sinclair, and illustrations by John Coulthart, but due to the timing of the publication; 2018 marks the 140th anniversary of Hodgson's birth and the 100th anniversary of his death in addition to the fact that Hodgson has slowly but surely seen a renewed interest and increasing popularity amongst readers.

Let this conversation not only serve as a fitting coda then to this Year of Hodgson but also to further discussion.

Sam Gafford: One hundred years after his death at the Fourth Battle of Ypres in April 1918, William Hope Hodgson still struggles for critical and popular acknowledgment. Despite his status as a pioneer of horror and science fiction literature, he still remains unknown to many. But, thanks to the efforts of people like Brian Showers and Swan River Press,

Hodgson's name stretches farther and farther each year.

Hodgson (1877–1918) lived a remarkable life by anyone's standards. He ran away to sea at the age of thirteen and joined the Merchant Marine. For ten years he sailed the seas in what has become known as the last great age of sailing ships. He circumnavigated the globe several times, saved a crewman from shark-infested waters off the coast of Australia, was a pioneer of the very early science of maritime photography (credited with taking the first pictures of 'stalk lightning,' which is a phenomenon where lightning rises from the ocean during a storm up into the sky), and even achieved his Second Mate's certificate. However, bitter and disillusioned, Hodgson left the sea in 1900, never to return other than in his writings.

Back home in Blackburn, Hodgson opened a "School for Physical Culture." The "school" closed shortly after a controversial attempt by Hodgson to shackle the great magician Houdini—Houdini would describe it as the most brutal treatment he had ever received during his many handcuff challenges. Shortly thereafter, Hodgson began writing. His writing 'life' was brief. He wrote for basically only fourteen or so years from 1902 to 1916, when he joined the British Army to fight in World War I. There is evidence to indicate that his best and greatest work was done early during this time and probably completed around 1905–06. This would include his four novels, the stories of occult detective Thomas Carnacki, and several of his best-known short stories such as "The Voice in the Night."

Despite his raw imagination and talent, Hodgson never attained bestseller status, as indicated by the drop in the quality of his publishers as time went on. Although his work often received favorable critical notices, he never caught the fancy of the reading majority—a circumstance that perplexed and depressed him. While contemporary writers like Algernon Blackwood, Arthur Machen, and others were being embraced as the giants in a new literary field, Hodgson was left by the wayside.

Illustration © 2018 by John Coulthart, used by permission.

The joey Zone: Even giants such as these need perennial literary renewal. Lovecraft, as another example, went from Arkham House to Ballantine, with smaller imprints in between, before finally gaining a more permanent "list status" with Penguin Classics.

SG: Of his four novels, *The House on the Borderland* is perhaps Hodgson's most famous and influential work. Telling the story of a recluse in a house in remote Ireland via the discovery of a lost manuscript found among ruins, it is a piece of literature that stubbornly refuses categorization, summation, or even examination. In parts adventure novel and other parts consciousness-expanding science fiction, it has captivated readers ever since its first publication in 1908. It is a work that can mean many different things to many different readers, and each interpretation can be just as valid and worthy as the next. It has influenced many writers and received accolades from others, including H. P. Lovecraft in his groundbreaking essay "Supernatural Horror in Literature." According to the official Hodgson bibliography, published in *William Hope Hodgson: Voices from the Borderland* (Hippocampus Press, 2014), it has appeared in no fewer than 45 editions, which doesn't even include the many print-on-demand versions of dubious and questionable merit.

TjZ: Artist John Coulthart was interviewed in issue 9 of the magazine *Esoterra* in 2000. He brought up the idea of doing "an illustrated edition of *The House on the Borderland* (originally for Savoy Press) . . . intending that this should be as definitive as we can make it." On his seminal blog *Feuilleton* in 2010 he followed up that with: "I've been talking for years about doing a series of illustrations for HoTB and may yet make good on that threat: *never say never.*"

In other words . . . we've been waiting eighteen years for this!

SG: All these previous publishers, and anyone in the future considering reprinting *The House on the Borderland,* can now pack it in and give up the ghost, because Swan River Press has produced the best version ever. There is no need for any other, for none will match this triumph.

Beginning with an effective and atmospheric cover by John Coulthart (and, believe me, most previous editions *don't* have appropriate covers, such as the 1977 Manor paperback with an ear of corn in the foreground and a farm scene in the back), you know that this is a production of superior quality. Here is a publisher who is giving the work the respect and dedication it deserves.

TjZ: There are a LOT of deluxe versions of Lovecraft, Poe, etc. THIS HoTB is really. . . incomparable. *The bar has been raised on Hodgsonian illustration.* Collectors of the many editions of *The House* such as Gafford (and Brian Showers) call this . . . an affliction. We would posit the term *affection*.

SG: The famed writer Alan Moore (who is himself a Hodgson fan and has included Carnacki in his *League of Extraordinary Gentlemen* series) provides a thought-provoking introduction to the novel that effectively summarizes Hodgson's life and places the novel in the perspective of both its own time and today. Moore makes the brilliant observation that *The House on the Borderland* is a literary equivalent of the recent "found footage" film genre and discusses it as a piece of psychogeography. Moore also wrote an introduction to the graphic novel adaptation of the novel by Richard Corben (Vertigo, 2000) which is worth checking out, but his essay here is new and written specifically for this edition.

Next comes a beautifully designed text with stunning artwork by John Coulthart. It would be easy for me to say that, so far, none have come as close as Coulthart in capturing the spirit and terror of Hodgson's writing. The very first plate is especially stunning and evocative.

TjZ: The illustration for the "Searching of the Gardens" chapter is reminiscent of the work of Thomas Cole in its quiet yet sinister sublimity. This edition's images go beyond the usual delineations of swine things into the visionary tableaus encountered by the narrator.

SG: All Coulthart's illustrations should be collected and printed as a separate portfolio of prints. A limited-edition run of the book also includes a CD of accompanying music by Jon Mueller, which provides an appropriately moody addition to the experience.

TjZ: An elephant folio would do justice to the detail! The illustrator had quite an "Annus Mirabilis" in 2017: as of December, John "only" did eighty-seven or so illustrations including Editorial Alma's Spanish edition of Edgar Allan Poe, with definitive versions of the tales that surpass some images by Wilfred Satty and even Harry Clarke.

In a way, this presentation of *The House* could be compared to Savoy Books' edition of David Lindsay's *A Voyage to Arcturus,* the plus being that he fully illustrated the text as well. Coulthart said of the binding: "Nothing elaborate, a solarized collage of Gothic window and a starry sky"—yet that more than succeeds in emphasizing the cosmic dimension as much as the horror. The latter usually overwhelms the former when it comes to illustration of this work, even though it's only about half of the novel. It is *almost* a crime then that a dust wrapper covers the boards on this!

SG: Finishing the book is a reprint of an essay by Iain Sinclair that appeared in an earlier edition of *The House on the Borderland*. Sinclair's thoughts are interesting and provocative and, although I'm not sure I agree with them, worth reading. I am not entirely convinced by Sinclair's theory that underlying the plot is an element of incest between the narrator and his sister. Perhaps this is because in most of his fiction Hodgson portrays women as a 'romantic ideal,' a damsel to be rescued. This is certainly true when we consider that the novel was written early in Hodgson's career, when his conceptions of women were perhaps a little naïve and unworldly. It is interesting to consider that these opinions appear to have changed by 1916 when, during his Captain Gault series, women are portrayed as manipulative and dishonest. In any case, Sinclair's comments here show that there is much to study in both the novel and Hodgson's attitude toward women.

TjZ: All William Hope Hodgson's work engenders *depth:* in discussion toward differing interpretations. The perennial renewal of his visionary art is justified in following years as well as this one. In other words, this is just the start of the conversation on Hope!

SG: I wish that all Hodgson's novels could receive such an appreciative and affectionate reprint. How wonderful it would be to see them lined up on my bookshelf as the pinnacle of Hodgson editions! For now, we need to be grateful to Brian Showers and Swan River Press for this handsome volume of one of the most truly unique novels in the history of horror *or* science fiction.

Adam Nevill: The Sense of Dread

S. T. Joshi

British writer Adam Nevill (b. 1969) has published seven substantial weird novels and two exquisitely produced self-published collections of short stories; but because only four of the novels have appeared in the United States, Nevill does not seem to have as much of a following on this side of the water as he deserves. His work is deeply infused with allusions to the writings of Lovecraft, Arthur Machen, M. R. James, and others, and more broadly with a refusal—perhaps inspired by the examples of these authors—to descend into conventional supernaturalism by the use of standard vampires, ghosts, and other common tropes. Even when such tropes are used, they are revitalized with innovative features and treatments. Within his novels, while quite lengthy and to some degree aimed at a popular audience (a common blurb on his books is that he is "Fast becoming Britain's answer to Stephen King"—a dubious tribute indeed), Nevill reveals an admirable ability to convey a profound sense of dread, in which those exposed to the horror are simultaneously baffled as to its exact nature, properties, and psychological motivations and terrified at its immense power to create mayhem, perhaps on a worldwide scale.

Nevill's first novel, *Banquet for the Damned* (2004), takes place at the University of St. Andrews in southeastern Scotland. It focuses on a book, *Banquet of the Damned,* written in the 1930s by a now ageing professor of religion, Eliot Coldwell, that appears to speak of pagan entities and rituals. Various students and other residents of the town turn up dead, their bodies hideously mutilated. Suspicion focuses on Coldwell's assistant, a young woman named Beth, who either is a vampire or believes herself to be one; but more potent and anomalous creatures appear to be lurking. Without giving away too much, we are in fact dealing with a coven of witches and, in particular, with a witch's familiar named the Brown Man, whose emergence toward the end of the novel results in a spectacular denouement.

Banquet for the Damned is a rich tapestry of supernatural and psychological horror. Nevill has drawn upon his wide reading of classic supernatural fiction for some phases of his novel. But we are puzzled by a few unexplained features. Nevill is somewhat vague in his description of the Brown Man—perhaps by design, as the creature only manifests itself fully at the end. But why and how Beth turns into a vampire is never clarified. There is a suggestion that her body is possessed by some entity, but this idea is never fully elucidated. But the greatest flaw in *Banquet for the Damned* is excessive verbosity. The novel could have benefited from being pruned by at least a quarter, perhaps a third. It becomes particularly bogged down by prolixity in the lead-up to the climactic scene—the exploration of the basement of Eliot's cottage—which in itself is indeed one of the more striking set-pieces of supernatural menace in contemporary fiction.

The Ritual (2011), adapted as a film in 2017, takes us to Sweden, where four school friends, now in their mid-thirties, are on a hiking trip. They are referred to as Hutch, Luke, Phil, and Dom. One by one, however, they are killed in some mysterious and nameless fashion, until only Luke is left. He in turn is captured by two men and one woman who call themselves Fenris, Loki, and Surtr. The men are devotees of black metal music and are in a band called Blood Frenzy. Fenris claims that he and his band worship Odin, going on to state, "In this wood is a real God." Are they—or the old woman who resides with them—preparing to sacrifice Luke in order to effect the return of the god?

The Ritual, although as long as or longer than *Banquet for the Damned,* is considerably more compact and tightly knit than its predecessor, although it too could perhaps have been cut down slightly. Large portions of it—especially the lengthy episode where Luke is the captive of the crazed young people in the cabin—read like an extended *conte cruel.* Luke seems on several occasions to be on the verge of escaping from his imprisonment, only to be recaptured. And the image of his physical degradation—especially after suffering his head wound, which his captors do little to treat—makes for almost unbearably grim reading.

Whether the portrayal of the four Englishmen is distinct enough to be fully satisfying is another matter. At one stage it is revealed that the apparent prosperity of both Phil and Dom is a sham, as they have both been abandoned by their wives and are in financial trouble. The men's discussions of their personal lives are scattershot and unsystematic, but nonetheless paint an occasionally vivid picture of lives that have inexorably diverged from the optimism and bravado of youth to the stolidity of early middle age. The portrayal of Loki and his compatriots is in some ways more vivid, since a clear conflict between them and their captive, Luke, brings each of the figures into sharper focus. And the shadowy presence of the old woman, never named, is a triumph of sinister suggestion.

Last Days (2012) is the story of a young filmmaker, Kyle Freeman, who is commissioned by Max Solomon, the head of a London company called Revelation Productions, to make a documentary relating to the circumstances surrounding the death of a woman who called herself Sister Katherine, who gathered a band of devoted followers, many of whom (including Katherine herself) perished in a place called the Temple of the Last Days near Phoenix, Arizona, in 1975. The project requires Freeman to travel throughout England, France, and the United States to ascertain exactly what happened to the cult—and, specifically, whether anything truly supernatural occurred. Freeman finds plenty of evidence of that, including the existence of shadowy entities called the Blood Friends, who seek to return from a state of incorporeality to that of fully living creatures by possessing the bodies of certain hapless human beings.

Nevill has meticulously worked out the details and sequence of this complex, richly textured, and multifaceted work. It is true that certain parts of the novel drag a bit, as there is excessive attention devoted to the filming of certain segments of the documentary on which Kyle and Dan are at work; but aside from this, the novel is tightly constructed, and even minor characters are vividly realized. Kyle Freeman must persevere in a baffling pursuit of natural and supernatural horrors whereby he alternately believes his death is imminent and that he will attain fame by verifying the existence of paranormal forces with his documentary.

As in Nevill's other novels, many of the scenes of supernatural terror are masterfully handled. The gradualness with which Nevill reveals the true nature of the Blood Friends creates exquisite suspense and fascination throughout the narrative, as readers attempt to piece together the bewildering array of supernatural elements that seem to be exhibiting themselves. As the various cultists interviewed by Kyle are killed or mutilated, in a seemingly systematic fashion, it begins to appear as if no one can survive the predations of the skeleton-like entities.

Lost Girl (2015) is a novel of a very different sort. This incredibly grim dystopian tale, set in the year 2053, is a poignant fusion of global terror—brought on by the crippling effects of climate change—with the searing emotional agony of a single individual. We are introduced to a man who, throughout this long novel, never receives a name but is called only "the father"—because, two years earlier, he had experienced the kidnapping of his four-year-old daughter (herself never named) as she was playing in his front garden of their house in Torquay. The father now seeks to use whatever means are necessary to rescue his daughter from her captors.

This intensely personal drama takes place while both England and much of the world is facing the breakdown of the political, legal, social, and moral standards that define civilization in the wake of climate change. It is a time of intense and unrelenting heat, and in many regions the forces of the local and national government have given way to ruthless criminal gangs. The father's relentless pursuit of his daughter's captors leads him through a violence-filled world where he himself must adopt the bloody ways of his enemies to achieve his objective.

The novel's overarching backdrop of a world consumed by multiple layers of horror and tragedy in the wake of climate change and the imminent collapse of civilization that it has brought in its wake is what is truly memorable. In an afterword, Nevill points to the numerous treatises on the subject he has read, many of which have confirmed his "suspicions about what awaits us in this interconnected world's future," and his simultaneous portrayal of a single man's trauma with the trauma facing the planet is deft and memorable.

If Nevill is to be faulted for anything, it is that he does not seem to have adequately portrayed any significant advances in technology that the decades from now until 2053 would have yielded. The father does use something called "stun gas" to incapacitate his foes from time to time, but otherwise he is still using good old-fashioned pistols or assault rifles to blow away his antagonists, and still uses cellphones, the Internet, and other devices we are familiar with today. Perhaps Nevill wishes to suggest that, in the wake of civilization's near-collapse, technological advance is neither possible nor welcome. In any event, *Lost Girl* is an unforgettable dystopian novel—perhaps only on the borderline of weird fiction, and more aptly a mingling of science fiction with the crime novel. But at a minimum it demonstrates the widening range of Nevill's novelistic output.

I have left little room for a discussion of Nevill's short story collections, *Some Will Not Sleep* (2016) and *Hasty for the Dark* (2017), both issued under his own imprint, Ritual Limited. They are exquisite examples of fine book production, but their contents are a tad uneven. Nevill seems more comfortable working in the novella or novel form, for these allow him to portray his characters over an extended compass and also to weave complex narrative threads into a generally satisfying whole.

Nevill's writing is far from perfect. At times his prose can be dismayingly slipshod. Aside from succumbing to the solecisms now distressingly common among today's writers (split infinitives, misuse of "like" for "as" or "as if," etc.), he makes awkward errors such as "sight" for "site," "bare" for "bear" (as a verb), and so on. Evidently his copy editors in Britain are incapable of correcting these errors. In general, however, his prose is smooth-flowing and at times eloquent. In several of his novels, it is not entirely clear whether the array of supernatural manifestations can all be harmonized into a coherent whole. This point may be related to the substantial length of most of his novels: there is some reason to believe that Nevill at times loses track of the multifarious details and plot elements he throws out, failing to unify them at the end. (One of the novels I didn't read—*No One Gets Out Alive* [2014]—is a whopping 628 pages.)

But overall, Adam Nevill's novels are refreshing in their vivid contemporaneousness, their crisply realized characters, the deftness of their execution of a complex and many-stranded plot, and most particularly in the originality of their supernatural scenarios. The author displays an unerring sense of those hints and details that are most likely to evoke terror and dread in the reader, and he exhibits the skill to elicit those emotions without descending into crude bloodletting. Nevill's subsequent career is well worth watching.

Horrifying Abnormality
of the Mundane

Fiona Maeve Geist

TIM WAGGONER. *Dark and Distant Voices: A Story Collection*. Mount Juliet, TN: Nightscape Press, 2018. 230 pp. $15.99 tpb. ISBN: 978-1-938644-25-2.

Dark and Distant Voices is the fifth collection from Tim Waggoner and my first exposure to him. The collection itself consists of nineteen stories that share some stylistic similarities while illustrating depth and flourish in what could have been a repetitive collection. Most of the stories concern the intrusion of surreal, horrific, macabre and, importantly, unexplained events into the mundane. This injection of strange elements into normal interaction—going to the DMV, canoeing on a lake, flying on a plane, possibly seeing your daughter skipping school, picking up strangers and giving them a ride—showcases three important strengths to Waggoner's writing in this collection:

- An attentiveness to mundane detail that allows the creeping horror/weirdness/unreality of the situation to unfold effectively, including having characters who are more than a vehicle for the reversal.

- A refusal to provide extensive explanation that would undercut the interesting *consequences* of the infusion of these elements into the narrative.

- A frequent fixation on providing an exploration of the consequences of this alteration to mundanity. This is, to borrow his own words, "about as funny as a straight razor slicing across the surface of an eyeball and only slightly less painful."

There is something really interesting about the absurdity of the premises—the dead calling their family members, the sun being a devouring predator, a plane animating and devouring the lives of others as a bird of prey—which are navigated in a manner that makes the absurdity work.

That is, the stories are not focused on the mechanism of

horror, although the horror element is quite strong, but on the way the elements warp the experiences of his characters. What lends gravitas to this proceeding is the focus on memories, traumas, and inner states of the narrator, providing a depth to the experience that immerses the reader in the story itself. Of particular interest is the story "Sky Watching," an account of a paranormal experience interspersed with reflections upon horror.

As Waggoner notes in "Sky Watching," there are particular perceptions and expectations of horror writers and, by extension, horror writing. The story unfolds at a horror author's reading on Halloween that involves prolonged reflection on horror itself conjoined with the more mundane frustrations of a writer and parent. As Waggoner's ostensible double describes horror itself:

> People who aren't into horror sometimes think horror writers are obsessed with the darkest aspects of human existence, that we get off wallowing in blood, violence, and death. But the truth is more complex. There's a complicated attraction/repulsion to the darker aspects of existence that's almost impossible to explain.

This attraction/repulsion element deserves some reflection. Haunting the collection are feelings of trauma, dread, and anxiety.

"For She Is Fearfully and Wonderfully Made" is an excellent demonstration of these elements. The horror reveal in the story is barely a paragraph, but the story itself is framed around a father's anxiety that he has seen his daughter skipping school and compounding anxieties about how people would perceive him trying to catch a glance of a young girl to determine the reality of his anxiety alongside recalling trope horror elements regarding his daughter—remembering her crushing a ladybug and, most relevant to the final reveal, finding her copy of *Deformations,* a grimoire of horrifying photography. As the narrator states, the book itself delivers on its titular promise with "Malformed features, extra limbs, distorted orifices, mutated genitals . . . Each page is more disturbing than the last, and what's worse, the most shocking pages have been dog-eared for future reference." The conclusion is eerie and opaque; the hybrid of more traditional horror child elements with mundane anxieties or parenting elevates the story.

"The Talking Dead" follows a dissimilar trajectory, hypothesizing how the world would unravel if the dead contacted us simply to berate, shame, castigate, and ridicule their families. The narrator watches civilization wind down as people increasingly avoid communication that could allow the dead to continue their tirades. As the narrator notes:

> The dead know, all right. They know what really waits for us all on the other side, and once they found a way to do so, they were only too happy to share that knowledge with those who were still alive. And every time we turned away from one avenue of communication, they switched to another to make sure their message got through.

The story climaxes with an act of self-mutilation and a personal revelation by the narrator that living is just a cocoon for death as he prepares to finish off the living.

Other stories explore territory closer to bizarro fiction, such as "Blood and Bone," a workplace performance review in a world of werewolves. "Weeper" treads similarly bizarre territory concerning obsessiveness, refusal to let go, and a husband living with static versions of his wife and daughter maintaining his world through the Sisyphean task of murdering and disposing of copies of himself that seek to take over his position in the unchanging family. Overall, the stories cover a wide range; even if certain thematic conceits or framing methods reappear, the work never becomes stale.

A pertinent revelation bookends "Sky Watching" after the narrator investigates an abandoned observatory and is pursued by eerie glowing figures. While at the start of the story he identifies horror as something Ligottian related to hopelessness and the absence of meaning, finding himself transfixed in the gaze of a "Lev-*eye*-athan" changes the narrator's evaluation. As he reflects:

> Do I feel insignificant? Who wouldn't feel that way under the circumstances? It's only—if the word can apply in a situation like this—natural.
>
> But here's the thing: I feel the opposite. I feel significant,

more so than I ever have in my life. At this precise instant I feel like the most important person on the planet. Hell, the most important person who's ever lived in the entire history of the human race, from the first primitive ape-like mammal scratching itself in a tree to the theoretical physicist who's discovered irrefutable proof of a new quantum particle. More important than any king, martyr, explorer or genocidal despot. . . . [I had answered the question] wrong earlier tonight. I only thought I was afraid that existence was intrinsically without meaning. But I've discovered something so much worse. *Everything* has meaning.

This inversion of the hackneyed Lovecraftian revelation of a meaningless universe beset by unfathomable terrors, intrinsically arguing that it is meaning itself at the root of horror, feels like an excellent summary of the collection itself. The terror in these stories is not the focus; unknowable beasts and monsters may show up, but there is something far more terrible about their appearance in the context of people's loneliness, depression, anxiety, dread, and aspirations. "The Goggan," for example, has a heavily fairytale or folklore feeling that would slot nicely into *The Twilight Zone,* but it is the horror of the narrator's indifference to harming his ex, knowing the devastation he would bring about through his selfish actions and not his replacing an oracular monster, that drives the horror.

Not every story is equally successful. Although the collection is dominated by stronger stories, some feel too lacking in character depth to execute the premise successfully. For example, "Lover Come Back to Me" suffers from two characters who are too paper-thin to experience much of anything, and demonstrates what happens when this style isn't executed as well as Waggoner's other stories are. Specifically, two unpleasant and unsympathetic people bicker and argue before a reveal that doesn't connect because there isn't weight to the interaction. This instance sticks out in particular, although certainly the individuals and relationships populating the collection as a whole are probably not universally interesting to every reader. However, with this caveat, the collection is overwhelmingly made up of stories that showcase someone who has mastered a particular style exploring a range within it. This is a strong collection with wonderful illustrations for each piece by Luke Spooner that really capture their mood. It is a recommendable purchase for those interested in work straddling the surreal terrain between contemporary weird fiction and bizarro that manages to carry off mundane emotional states without being saccharine or dull.

Stephen King: Fast Food or Five Star?

James Arthur Anderson

Stephen King began his writing career in a most humble fashion, writing short stories for men's skin magazines that paid him modest checks, which, along with his day job, barely paid the bills. His dream, of course, was to publish novels, but in the 1970s, when the horror genre consisted of just a handful of books, it seemed impossible to imagine that the author of fiction published in *Cavalier* and *Adam* would one day be one of the world's top selling authors, a brand name in his own right. Possibly even more difficult to believe would be the fact that King, who once described his own work as "the literary equivalent of a Big Mac and fries" (*Different Seasons* 506), would find his work written about and discussed by professors like me with alphabet soup after their names. I find it doubtful that King himself could have imagined receiving awards from the National Book Foundation and from the president of the United States, let alone be selected to guest-edit *The Best American Short Stories 2007*.

Admittedly, King is not embraced by all, or even most literary scholars. However, despite his self-deprecation, "Bestsellasaurus Rex" (Beahm 7), King has come a long way since he received his first check for *Carrie,* a manuscript that his wife Tabitha rescued from the trash.

Over the years, King's critics have been harsh. Esteemed scholar and critic Harold Bloom accuses King of the "Dumbing Down of American Letters" ("Dumbing"), claims his books are "not literary at all" ("Afterword" 207), and that "the triumph of the genial King is a large emblem of the failures of American Education ("Introduction" 2). Dwight Allen has recommended not reading King "unless you are maybe fifteen and have made it clear to your teachers and everybody else that you aren't going to touch that literary 'David Copperfield kind of crap' with a ten-foot pole" ("My Stephen King Problem"). Noted horror critic S. T. Joshi writes that

King "delivers a predictable effect on his readers, in the same manner as McDonald's or Budweiser" (*Unutterable Horror* 626) and that "the great proportion of his work will, as with so many of the bestsellers of prior ages, lapse into oblivion with the passage of time" (*Unutterable Horror* 632).

So why have the critics been so severe and dismissive of an author who has, over a forty-year career, become an icon of popular culture? There are a number of reasons, some simple, and some more complex.

First of all, Stephen King writes bestsellers and there is a pronounced critical bias on the part of scholars towards anything that appeals to the masses. As Darrell Schweitzer noted in 1985, "King seems to have pleased almost everyone except conventional mainstream literary critics, who are immediately suspicious of anything which isn't theirs and which is successful" (*Discovering Stephen King* 5). And while book reviewers and the reading public in general have accepted and even embraced the validity of "pop culture," the academy has been slow to catch up with this trend. As McAleer and Perry admit in the introduction to their 2014 anthology of criticism, "it is hard to not begin from a defensive standpoint when engaged in a sustained critical piece of scholarship that address King" (2). Part of this is a belief by many academics that scholars are the arbitrators of good taste (a topic I will address in more detail later) and that ordinary non-scholars need to be told what is best for them; scholars establish the literary canon and then feed it to students through the development of a curriculum of literature that is included in the accepted textbooks. In the past this idea has had lamentable consequences in the dismissal and ignoring of female authors, authors of color, and other underrepresented peoples and cultures while instead privileging "dead white males" in school curriculums. My own public high school experience, for example, completely ignored the Harlem Renaissance, but favored Longfellow and Kipling.

The scorn for bestselling fiction means that a good number of educators and scholars don't even read it, let alone teach it. In "Canon Construction Ahead," Kelly Chandler cites a case of English teachers excluding King from the curriculum without even having read his works: "Refusing to read King seemed like a point of honor, a finger in the dike between popular culture and the classroom" (112). In her book *Teaching Stephen King*, Alissa Burger notes, "King has often been dismissed out of hand as just a genre writer and in this assessment his popularity has frequently been marshalled against him on the argument that fiction that appeals to the masses cannot be simultaneously literary" (3). Dwight Allen, a self-professed "snob," admits that he refused to read King's books and had an aversion to horror fiction. His analysis of Stephen King as a writer is based on four novels that he reluctantly read; he never got around to reading what critics consider King's best works, including "The Body," *The Green Mile,* and *Lisey's Story,* but bases much of his condemnation of King on his reading of *Christine* and *The Girl Who Loved Tom Gordon,* certainly not vintage Stephen King books. Though he claims to have read King with "an open mind," I think that he doth protest too much, especially as he whines about the lack of sales of "literary" novels, the kind that he and his friends write—perhaps a bit of the green-eyed monster?

Another reason King is eschewed by mainstream scholars is because he not only writes genre fiction, as has been alluded to in the critical disdain of bestselling authors, but horror, the worst form of genre fiction. As Bloom has said, "King . . . emerges from an American tradition one could regard as sub-literary: Poe and H. P. Lovecraft" (207). Of course, those who study horror fiction disagree with Bloom: "Horror literature is capable of expressing elements of the human condition in ways philosophical discourse often cannot," says Jacob Held in his introduction to *Stephen King and Philosophy* (6).

Perhaps the major reason that King has been either ignored or attacked by mainstream critics, though, lies in the nature of critical study itself. In virtually all schools and even most colleges, literature is taught using simplistic and outdated theories that privilege style over story. Thus, in most literature classes, students still use American New Criticism (which, ironically, dates back to I. A. Richards in 1929) as their main tool in analyzing literature. This method is easy to teach and assumes that there is a "meaning" in the text that must be meticulously pulled out. Students, therefore, duteously examine symbolism, theme, setting, characterization, etc. in order to find this hidden meaning and parrot it back to their teacher in a five-paragraph essay.

Academic critics privilege style over story, and thus favor stories with poetic language, stories that take the familiar and make it seem extraordinary, rather than speculative fiction, which makes the fantastic seem realistic. Dwight Allen, one of King's harshest critics, said, "Among the things I hope for when I open a book of fiction is that each sentence I read will be right and true and beautiful, that the particular music of those sentences will bring me a pleasure I wouldn't be able to find the exact equivalent of in another writer." And, no, for the most part, King does not write the beautiful language Allen is looking for. His use of brand names, common language, slang, blue-collar characters, and focus on story over style has been widely criticized by those seeking a poetic narrative. Critics from various schools of thought have attacked American New Criticism, from Marxist critics such as György Lukács, who examine culture and ideology in narrative (17), to psycho-linguistic critics such as Michelle Scalise Sugiyama, who make a strong argument, based on neuroscience, that story and action determine a narrative's success (183).

As I have said earlier, old-school critics like Harold Bloom have set themselves up as the arbiters of good taste. Bloom, for example, has not only attacked contemporary popular authors (Stephen King, Anne Rice, and J. K. Rowling among others have been his targets), but believes that all literature has been merely a copy of a copy: "The great poets of the English Renaissance are not matched by their Enlightened descendants, and the whole tradition of the post-Enlightenment, which is Romanticism, shows a further decline in its Modernist and post-Modernist heirs" ("Anxiety" 1800). According to Bloom's theory, then, every story is a copy of one made before it and, like a photocopy of a photocopy, after enough duplication, literature will be reduced to a blank page. Since the classics were written, each generation has watered down the last—hence, King and others are now "dumbing down" literature.

The problems with this argument are many, but perhaps the most obvious is that Bloom, a psychoanalytic critic by his own definition, is working with Freudian theories that have been proven to be obsolete (Carroll 37). Furthermore, this "dumbing down" of America is also untrue. As Boyd has noted, "despite complaints about the dumbing down of culture . . . no epidemic of intellectual obesity threatens us, and . . . IQ levels have risen with each decade since they were first measured" ("Evolutionary Theories" 154). Gottschall reminds us that "the novel is a young genre, but for a century critics have been writing and rewriting its obituary" (177).

Traditional criticism looks at literature in a way that does not favor genre writers like Stephen King, who place story above style. Many of these critics prefer artistry to story and celebrate books that no one reads, perhaps for their snob appeal. In fact, it sometimes seems that modern poets and literary writers are writing for each other and not for readers at all. Gottschall sums it up well: "novelists who target highbrow readers shouldn't complain when those are the only readers they get" (179). Many of these novels that the critics rave about contain little or no plot, and subscribe to the Gertrude Stein philosophy of stories where "nothing much happens." Says Gottschall, "nothing much happens, and aside from English professors, no one much wants to read them" (55).

A number of scholars also criticize postmodern theory as being overly political at the expense of narrative. According to Carroll, poststructuralism currently dominates the academy and, by blending deconstructionism, Freudianism, and Marxism, "in its political aspect . . . treats . . . normative intellectual, moral, and social structures within Western Culture as fraudulent and oppressive" (17). Thus, politics and culture become more important than the works themselves, and authors may be attacked on their beliefs rather than on the quality of their work, a situation that Lovecraft scholars are all too familiar with. Boyd says that there are more fruitful ways of looking at literature than "analyzing how ideology . . . determines narrative" (*Origin* 130), and while I believe that analyzing the culture in which a work was created is a useful tool both in understanding a narrative and in enlightening readers about society past and present, I do not think it should be the dominating factor in determining artistic merit.

So, if the mainstream scholars have been so harsh, how do we account for Stephen King's unparalleled popular success as a writer of horror fiction? Does King's "Constant Reader" lack literary taste? The answer may lie not in the traditional realms of the literature departments of the academy, but in the fields of evolutionary psychology, linguistics, and neuroscience. According to the latest scholars working in these areas, story and narrative developed as a result of human evolution: storytelling as a trait has enabled *Homo sapiens* to be a more successful species. Storytelling is one of the oldest forms of art, and it has developed as an adaptive function (Sugiyama 177). According to Boyd:

> Narrative arises from the advantages of communication in social species. It benefits audiences, who can choose better what course of action to take on the basis of strategic information, and it benefits tellers, who earn credit in the social information exchange and gain in terms of attention and status. That combination of benefits, for the teller and the told, and the intensity of social monitoring in our species, explain why narrative has become so essential to human life. (*Origin* 176)

This importance of story over style is King's trademark and certainly explains his popular success as a best-selling author. "In fiction, the story value holds dominance over every other facet of the writer's craft; characterization, theme, mood, none of these things is anything if the story is dull," King says in his foreword to *Nightshift* (xx). According to Lisa Cron, humans are "wired for story," which means that "storytelling trumps beautiful writing every time" (20). Gottschall says that "we are, as a species, addicted to story" (xiv).

Research into narrative shows that King is correct in putting story first. As Richard Gerrig noted in 1993, readers are "transported by a narrative by virtue of performing that narrative" (2). With new technology, MRI studies of the brain in 2009 have confirmed this idea.

Using MRI studies of subjects reading stories, scientists from the Dynamic Cognition Laboratory at Washington University in St. Louis conclude that our brains simulate the action in the story, echoing it as we read. According to Nicole

Speer, Director of Operations of the Intermountain Neuroimaging Consortium:

> Readers use perceptual and motor representations in the process of comprehending narrated activity, and these representations are dynamically updated at points where relevant aspects of the situation are changing. Readers understand a story by simulating the events in the story world and updating their simulation when features of that world change. (quoted in Everding)

In other words, readers' brains are actually experiencing the actions of characters in a story "using brain regions that closely mirror those involved when people perform, imagine, or observe similar real-world activities" (Everding).

Modern literary critics are now combining cognitive psychology, brain science, and linguistics in order to help understand literature. Linguists and psychologists believe that the ability to learn language is "a distinct piece of the biological makeup of our brains" (Pinker 4) and that "the seemingly infinite flexibility and open-endedness of language is one of the hallmarks of the human species" (Ramachandran 160). Boyd, Carroll, Gottschall and others have taken this idea one step further to show that the ability to effectively tell and comprehend story and narrative is an evolutionary adaptation that has enabled humans to become the dominant species on the planet. "Fiction allows our brains to practice reacting to the kinds of challenges that are, and always were, most crucial to our success as a species" (Gottschall 67). Language and the ability to tell stories is what distinguishes humans from every other species. Evolutionist critics, therefore, are looking at stories from the perspective of the master storyteller who can captivate audiences with fiction, films, or even video games that rely on narrative. This Darwinian approach privileges story over style and can help us understand the power of Stephen King's fiction. As Boyd explains, "an evolutionary approach . . . can show the problem situations of storytellers aiming to engage the attention of wide audiences" (*Origin* 389).

According to Joseph Carroll, "literature represents human motives and concerns, and it is written and read because it satisfies human needs" (107), and these motives and concerns can be thought of as "human universals." In literature, these universals are most often expressed in themes of survival and adventure, power and personal success, and love and romance (109). Thus, "the function of narrative . . . would appear to be the representation of the problems humans encounter in their lives and the constraints individuals struggle against in their efforts to solve them" (Sugiyama 186). Most of Stephen King's fiction involves the instinct for survival; in some novels, such as *The Stand* and *Cell,* it is not just the survival of the individual, but the survival of the human species itself, a Darwinian "universal" if there ever was one. Characters in all his books are not just confronted with normal, everyday problems, but struggle with extraordinary, conflicts that represent life and death. "Stories allow us to simulate intense experiences without actually having to live through them," says Cron. Alan Jacobs makes this point in his essay defending King:

> It is often said that such situations are unrealistic. This is incorrect; it conflates the unrealistic with the uncommon. People *do* confront such utterly decisive moments: A theater full of people in Aurora, Colorado confronted one quite recently, and some of them had only an instant to decide whether to save their own lives or protect the ones they loved. It doesn't get any more real than that. We can argue about whether Stephen King writes this kind of story well; but what's not really arguable, I think, is that such tales are worth writing and worth reading, even if beauty of language and subtlety of characterization get sacrificed along the way. Not all stories have to do the same things.

A good story, claims Boyd, must hold a reader's attention, "to attract and arouse an audience" (232), something that King certainly does well. Boyd acknowledges "the accomplishment of *any* storyteller who can secure an audience, wide or select, brief or enduring. There is nothing 'mere' about audience appeal" (*Origin* 253). The evolutionary critics agree that character and plot are the essential elements to achieve this goal, and that successful stories keep the reader wondering what will happen next. Roland Barthes linguistically describes the creation of action and suspense in terms of semiotic codes—the action code and the hermeneutic code (19). It is the action of the story and the "what happens next" that keep readers turning the pages. "You can celebrate *Finnegans Wake* as an act of artistic revolt, but you can't enjoy it as a story that takes you out of yourself and infects you with the need to know what happens next" (Gottschall 55).

Because of the latest advances in neuroscience, writers and those who educate them are, in fact, using brain science to "reverse engineer" stories, a process that allows authors to connect with their readers on a cognitive level. The idea is to take a successful story, like *The Godfather* or a Stephen King horror story, and work backward from the cognitive effect is has on the reader—in King's case, fear. This effect can be "hacked" and turned into a new, successful story according to these writing professors. Angus Fletcher, a core faculty member at Project Narrative at Ohio State University, uses this method to reverse engineer stories for film. Lisa Cron who teaches at UCLA is doing this for fiction.

It should be obvious that Stephen King has mastered the secret of attracting and keeping audiences over a career that has spanned forty years and more book sales than we can reasonably count. I would venture to say that his critics would happily trade royalty checks with him, even if it meant being thought of as a "master of post-literate prose" (quoted in Herron 22). Furthermore, despite condemnation of many mainstream academics, King is carving a name for himself as an author of some substance. Professors Tony Magistrale and Michael Collings have recognized King's skill for decades, and others are beginning to appreciate the depth of his work as well. In her Ph.D. dissertation, Jenifer Michelle D'Elia says that *The Stand* has "the depth expected of a serious literary work—themes, imagery, symbols, a certain 'arresting strangeness' and a resonation with readers . . . all the things a literary critic looks for" (149). Samuel Schuman, a literature professor at the University of North Carolina, posits that "King is a master of plot and setting; a skillful and self-conscious manipulator of the English language; a rather stern moralist; and a first-class creator of literary characters" (158).

Not only has King's output captivated millions, both with his fiction and film adaptations, but his works do exhibit more complexity than they are given credit for. He uses the popular novel to delve deeply into numerous important contemporary issues, including racism and the death penalty (*The Green Mile*), teenage suicide (*End of Watch*), and alcoholism (*The Shining*). According to Gottschall, "fiction seems to be more effective at changing beliefs than nonfiction, which is *designed* to persuade through argument and evidence" (150). King also explores a wide range of philosophical ideas in his fiction, such as Utilitarianism, Hindu philosophy, and the nature of evil (see Jacob Held). As a former English teacher, King references other authors in nearly all of his books.

As critics begin to re-examine Stephen King's books from the context of evolutionary literary theory, narratology, and cognitive psychology, all of which emphasize story, his fiction will be better understood and appreciated. Hoppenstand calls King "a consummate storyteller, perhaps the best storyteller of our era" (7). King, an avid reader himself, recognizes the delight that a good story can provide: "I want the ancient pleasure that probably goes back to the cave," he says ("Best" xvii).

Works Cited

Allen, Dwight. "My Stephen King Problem: A Snob's Notes." *Los Angeles Review of Books* (3 July 2012). lareviewofbooks.org/article/my-stephen-king-problem-a-snobs-notes/.

Barthes, Roland. *S/Z*. Trans. Richard Miller. New York: Hill & Wang, 1974.

Beahm, George. *The Stephen King Story*. Kansas City, MO: Andrews & McMeel, 1998.

Bloom, Harold. "Afterword." In *Bloom's Modern Critical Views: Stephen King*. Updated Edition. Ed. Harold Bloom. Philadelphia: Chelsea House, 2007. 207–8.

———. *The Anxiety of Influence* [extracts]. In *The Norton Anthology of Theory and Criticism,* ed. Vincent B. Leitch et al. New York: W. W. Norton, 2001. 1797–805.

———. "Dumbing Down American Readers." *Boston Globe* (24 September 2003).

———. "Introduction." In *Bloom's Modern Critical Views: Stephen King*. Updated Edition. Ed. Harold Bloom. Philadelphia: Chelsea House, 2007. 1–3.

Boyd, Brian. "Evolutionary Theories of Art." In *The Literary Animal,* ed. Jonathan Gottschall and David Sloan Wilson. Evanston, IL: Northwestern University Press, 2005. 147–76.

———. *On the Origin of Stories: Evolution, Cognition, and Fiction*. Cambridge, MA: Harvard University Press, 2009.

Burger, Alissa. *Teaching Stephen King: Horror, the Supernatural, and New Approaches to Literature*. New York: Palgrave MacMillan, 2016.

Carroll, Joseph. *Literary Darwinism*. New York: Routledge, 2004.

Chandler, Kelly. "Canon Construction Ahead." In *Reading Stephen King: Issues of Censorship, Student Choice, and Popular Literature,* ed. Brenda Muller Power et al. Orono, ME: NCTE, 1997. 105–11.

Cron, Lisa. *Wired for Story*. Berkeley, CA: Ten Speed Press, 2012.

Everding, Gerry. "Readers build vivid mental simulations of narrative situations, brain scans suggest." *The Source*. Washington University in St. Louis. 26 January 2009. source.wustl.edu/2009/01/readers-build-vivid-mental-simulations-of-narrative-situations-brain-scans-suggest/.

Gerrig, Richard J. *Experiencing Narrative Worlds: On the Psychological Activities of Reading*. New Haven, CT: Yale University Press, 1993.

Gottschall, Jonathan. *The Storytelling Animal*. Boston: Houghton Mifflin Harcourt, 2012.

Held, Jacob M., ed. *Stephen King and Philosophy*. Lanham, MD: Rowman & Littlefield, 2016.

Herron, Don. "Stephen King: The Good, the Bad, and the Academic." In *Bloom's Modern Critical Views: Stephen King*. Updated Edition. Ed. Harold Bloom. Philadelphia: Chelsea House, 2007. 17–40.

Hoppenstand, Gary. "On Stephen King." In *Critical Insights: Stephen King,* ed. Gary Hoppenstand. Pasadena, CA: Salem Press, 2011. 3–7.

Jacobs, Alan. "A Defense of Stephen King, Master of the Decisive Moment." *Atlantic* (24 July 2012). www.theatlantic.com/ entertainment/archive/2012/07/a-defense-of-stephen-king-master-of-the-decisive-moment/260187/.

Joshi, S. T. *Unutterable Horror: A History of Supernatural Fiction, Volume 2: The Twentieth and Twenty-first Centuries.* New York: Hippocampus Press, 2014.

King, Stephen. "Introduction." In *The Best American Short Stories 2007*. Boston: Houghton Mifflin, 2007.

———. *Different Seasons*. 1982. New York: Signet, 1998.

———. *Nightshift*. 1978. New York: Signet, 1979.

Lukács, Georg. *Realism in Our Time*. New York: Harper, 1969.

McAleer, Patrick, and Michael Perry. "Introduction: A More Subtle Macabre." In *Stephen King's Modern Macabre: Essays on the Later Works*. Jefferson, NC: McFarland, 2014. 1–8.

Pinker, Steven. *The Language Instinct*. New York: Harper Modern Classics, 2007.

Ramachandran, V. S. *The Tell-Tale Brain: A Neuroscientist's Quest for What Makes Us Human*. New York: W. W. Norton 2011.

Schuman, Samuel. "Taking King Seriously: Reflections on a Decade of Best-sellers." In *Critical Insights: Stephen King*, ed. Gary Hoppenstand. Pasadena, CA: Salem Press, 2011. 157–67.

Schweitzer, Darrell. "Introduction." In *Discovering Stephen King*, ed. Darrell Schweitzer. Mercer Island, WA: Starmont House, 1985.

Sugiyama, Michelle Scalise. "Reverse-Engineering Narrative: Evidence of Special Design." In *The Literary Animal*, ed. Jonathan Gottschall and David Sloan Wilson. Evanston, IL: Northwestern University Press, 2005. 177–96.

Signs of a Young Horror Master

Leigh Blackmore

JOSH MALERMAN. *Goblin: A Novel in Six Novellas*. Interior illustrations by Glenn Chadbourne. Introduction by James A. Moore. Northborough, MA: Earthling Publications, 2017. 376 pp. 500 numbered hc copies; 15 lettered copies. $50.00 hc. ISBN 978-0-9962118-5-7.

The owls are not what they seem.

Yes, I know that comes from *Twin Peaks,* but bear with me. Owls are also totemic creatures of darkness, wind and night which feature strongly in the book under consideration.

Josh Malerman is a previously unfamiliar name to me, but evidently he has received very good reviews for his previous works, *Bird Box* and *Black Mad Wheel,* which I confess to not having read. In this, his third (or maybe fourth?) book, a limited edition from Earthling Publications, Malerman lays claim to being one of the best young horror writers around. And that's not just because the book comes with some heavyweight praise from the likes of Clive Barker and Sarah Pinborough.

Now I have been reading horror for a very long time—approaching forty-five years. I have read the classics from the nineteenth century to all the great names of the twentieth century, and many of the obscure ones. After absorbing so much horror, it's sometimes a little difficult to work up enthusiasm for what a new writer might do. Will his tropes be the same old ones you've seen a thousand times before? Will his characters be convincing? And more importantly for me personally, will there be a frisson generated by the writer's use of suggestion and atmosphere, preferably shading into the supernatural, as opposed to simply a use of worn-out physical horror to evoke fear in the reader? I live in hopes.

I'm more than happy to report that I enjoyed every minute of reading *Goblin,* which takes its title from the name of a small town of Malerman's invention. Think Derry, think Castle Rock, think Oxrun Station, think Jerusalem's Lot, think Arkham, think every authentic-seeming dark and scary rain-haunted fictional locale you can conjure in your memory—and you will, on the one hand, have some idea of what Goblin is. And on the other hand, you won't. Because Goblin, despite being rooted in a well-trodden notion of *genius loci,* is a *fresh* place, created out of tautly stretched weird narrative fabric by a writer whose command of his craft could make older, more experienced writers weep.

Malerman's style is deceptively simple, and, at first I caught myself thinking that his tales were simply going to go through the motions. But then I began to find myself gripped, as the concision of the style had its way with me, and Malerman's taut, focussed, almost Hemingway-esque style pulled me deeper into his spooky conceptions. Certainly, there are evocative usages here that pay homage to iconic dark fantasy writers of the past—Ray Bradbury with his melancholic autumnal visions of the *Dark Carnival* period not least among them. At least one tale here conjures dark magic in a way reminiscent of Bradbury's *Something Wicked This Way Comes* and Joseph Payne Brennan's classic tale "Levitation." More than anything, Malerman's stories read like the work of a pared-down Stephen King—bringing to the page all the mesmerising weirdness of a King tale, but without the prolixity of King himself. I enjoy richly textured language in some writers, but I also go for work that cuts straight to the bone, and Malerman is definitely in the latter class.

One tale here features creepy hedges, and if that idea doesn't remind you of something straight out of *The Shining,* I'll be a monkey's uncle. But Malerman's strength is that his tales are simply somewhat redolent of these other writers—he is canny enough to tip his hat to such influences without letting his own material descend to mere pastiche. His original conceits are creepy enough, thank you, and he does a darned good job of keeping the reader white-knuckled over what might happen next in each individual set-piece.

The subtitle is somewhat disingenuous—what can a 'novel' in six novellas really be? This is clearly *not* a novel, for there is no focus on just a single set of protagonists, no narrative storyline that follows the primary characters and their challenges and development through the course of a story arc with clearly delineated first, second, and third acts, as one would find in most novels. *Goblin* is, in fact, a sextet of novellas. It is neither fish nor fowl—neither a novel nor a short story collection. But because Malerman has cleverly interconnected the pieces through references to the town's history, *Goblin* becomes a mythos. The place was founded by strange people to whom stranger things happened. And downright strange things *keep* happening in this sodden little offtrail town. It's just that kind of place.

The pieces most strongly linked together are the opening and closing novellas, in which a delivery driver who has been paid triple to deliver an unsettling box of *something* under strict conditions finds himself traveling that terrifying curve from the normal to the completely whacked-out over the course of his voyage. The conceit allows Malerman to provide a tasty closure to his set of novellas, rather like a concept album back in the day (think Pink Floyd's *Dark Side of the Moon* with its opening and closing tracks that thematically bracket the material contained between them, somehow making the whole more than simply the sum of its parts). I don't know if Malerman thought of it, but even the volume's title reminded me of my favorite horror movie metal band, the Italian group Goblin, who scored many of Dario Argento's *gialli* movies. Hey, it might not be relevant, but it's another potential resonance, and I liked it. (Malerman *may* have been canny enough to reference this group deliberately—he's a performing musician himself.)

I was well prepared not to like the American characters with whom Malerman peoples his tales. Probably this has to do again with my predilection for different styles of approach than Stephen King's folksiness. I am Australian, where the culture is somewhat different from the American Midwest, and tales of American strip malls and suburbia rarely cut it for me.

Imagine, then, my surprise at finding myself absolutely fascinated by the goings-on in the adolescent lives of certain characters here. I was caught up in the very real and emotionally affecting sense that friendship is worth doing almost anything for if you're a lonely and unappreciated youngster; the brooding atmosphere created by the well-chosen place-names, from the somewhat generic North Woods to the more sinister Perish Park and the aptly named river that snakes through the town. Malerman made me feel intimately involved with his characters, and their secrets, and their fuckups.

Bone-chilling horror, nightmares, fears both well-founded and imaginary, men who are so afraid of ghosts they remove all the interior walls from their apartment. Body parts, weird police, eerie owls, desperate relationships, disturbing owls, nameless things lurking in the shadows—this book has all the good stuff. And it's so well written you'll want to read it again. Or, as I'm going to do, seek out Malerman's other work. I hope that the author sets more stories in *Goblin*. It's a fascinating place, the locus of a plethora of events and characters that cries out for further exploration. While the owls are not what they seem, the town is even less so. As for the people who live there (or deliver there), if you like to be genuinely unsettled, you could spend time with no finer men and women.

Apart from the prose itself, the book is a quality production, to judge by Chadbourne's excellent line illustrations, included in the PDF from which I reviewed the volume. While the price of this book is steep, it is a highly recommended purchase for horror readers who may feel somewhat jaded with the usual fare. *Goblin*. A novel-in-parts. A fragment novel. A collection of interlinked novellas. Whatever you call it, go read it. You won't regret it.

When Unreality Becomes Too Unreal

Darrell Schweitzer

JOSH MALERMAN. *Unbury Carol*. New York: Del Rey, 2018. 362 pp. $27.00 hc. ISBN: 978-0-18016-3.

One has to admit that this novel has nowhere to go but up after an opening line that seems to be near gibberish. I still have not figured out precisely what the author is trying to say: "Harrows, situated at the northernmost point of the Trail, savored its distance from the meat of the rabid road."

The premise is one Poe could have used (and in various ways did): a woman goes into periodic "comas," which, in the absence of autopsies or embalming, may result in a premature burial. Rather than alert all her associates of her condition, she keeps it a secret. When John Bowie, a close friend and confidant, dies, the only person who apparently knows is her wicked husband Dwight, who married her for money and now sees an obvious opportunity to seize her estate. Another "coma" happens. He declares Carol dead and wants her buried right away. But one other person knows the truth, Carol's former lover, now turned outlaw; and a maid may suspect.

In the first few pages, this all seems to be taking place in a fog on a blank stage. Slowly details emerge. The husband travels by horse-drawn "coach," though I think the author means a buggy or carriage, since no driver is mentioned. There are no telephones or modern appliances mentioned. We are probably somewhere in the past. They've got telegraphs. The book's blurb hints that this is in the Old West, but this doesn't seem to be in the United States at all. The president is a woman named Coopersmith. We are not in any specific state, nor does there seem to be a landscape, either mountainous or prairie. There are no allusions to real places or historical events. The Civil War? President Grant? Indians and Indian wars? Nope. The maid addresses her mistress by her first name, Carol, which is not something a maid would do even today, let alone in 18-something.

That a young girl has lost her "bow" and evinces no interest in archery may be a typo, or an auto-correct making a nuisance of itself, but you can't be sure. Often little details (such as there are) and phrases seem wrong. The expression "pass" as opposed to "pass away" is used as a euphemism for dying. Older readers at least will remember that this has only come into use in the last decade or so. Nobody talked like that in 1980, let alone 1880.

The setting of the novel seems dominated by "the Trail," which appears to be tree-lined, and the only means of transit across this otherwise featureless world. An Illness stalks the land, though it is clear that Carol did not "die" of it.

Meanwhile the former lover, now outlaw, with the unlikely name of James Moxie, has learned of his lover's fate and comes riding to the rescue. But the wicked husband has hired a spectacular villain named Smoke, a man with tin legs below the knees. These legs are hollow and usually filled with oil, but Smoke has a gadget in his pockets that enables him to spill out oil through his heels, leaving an oil slick into which he can toss a match. At one point we see him burning a woman to death who is trapped in a crashed coach, just for the fun of it apparently, even though the loss of the oil causes him considerable discomfort and he immediately has to seek resupply.

Meanwhile Carol struggles in what she calls "Howltown," in her coma. Hero and villain are on their inevitable collision course. After that initial pratfall and considerable stumbling, the narrative develops a certain readability, moseying along without ever really becoming convincing or involving.

Given that Malerman has something of a track record (he won a Stoker for his first novel, *Bird Box,* in 2014), we have to assume that what we are seeing is the result of deliberate aesthetic decisions, and that, for all he demonstrates an uncertain ear for language, he must intend the effects found here. He may be trying for a kind of surreal/abstract/dreamlike "western" setting, like that of Stephen King's Gunslinger series. I can only say that I think this is a not a success, and the result merely robs the story of most of its potential power.

The Beauty and Horror of Home

Javier Martinez

ANDREW MICHAEL HURLEY. *Devil's Day*. New York: Houghton Mifflin Harcourt, 2018. 304 pp. $26.00 hc. ISBN 978-1-328-48988-3.

Andrew Michael Hurley's *Devil's Day* can be read as a contin- uation of the modern horror Gothic that emerged in the 1970s. A common theme in these works is the exodus of ur- ban protagonists who seek to escape the pressures of city life so that they may rejuvenate themselves in the pastoral land- scape of the British or American countryside. In so many of these stories any attempt to escape the modern world ends with the discovery, often too late, that the old world is a far worse place than the new. Variations on this theme are found in a film such as *The Wicker Man* (1973) and continue into the '80s with such novels as Bernard Taylor's *The Moonstone Sickness* (1982). Those works may be the most obvious exam- ples of the British lineage of *Devil's Day,* but it owes as much if not more to American counterparts of the same period, such as Thomas Tyron's *Harvest Home* (1973). But where the pro- tagonists of those other works seek refuge from the modern, the narrator and main character of *Devil's Day,* John Pente- cost, is under no such illusion. The responsibilities and diffi- culties of rural life are consistently highlighted throughout his telling. He comes to understand fully what it is he seeks, and it is through the process of finding it that he embraces the beauty and horror of home.

Devil's Day tracks the lives of the immediate Pentecost fam- ily: the novel's narrator John; his grandfather, referred to as the Gaffer; John's father Tom, or Dadda as he is most often called; John's wife Kat; and their blind son Adam. Other prominent characters in the novel include Bill and Laurel Dyer and their son Jeff, a small-time con; Angela Beasely, her adult daughter Liz, and Grace, Liz's daughter with Jeff. Together, this extended family inhabits the Endlands, which is near the village of Underclough in Briardale Valley. The bulk of the novel traces the relationship between John, a teacher in Suffolk, and his father and grandfather, sheep farmers, against the isolated, often freezing and rain-soaked backdrop of the British moors. The novel follows John's decision to return to his family ranch upon the occasion of his grandfather's death and assume those responsibilities that have historically been passed down through the Pentecost male line. His wife resists the idea, and with good reason as uncomfortable facts emerge and secrets are laid bare.

This scenario is hardly new, but the novel's strength lies in its superbly realized sense of place. An argument can be made that the landscape Hurley so richly describes is the novel's main character. Hurley has something of a poet's eye in his descriptions of a countryside that is as weird as it is recognizable. As in any Gothic, the names Hurley gives his locales resonate dread: Briardale, or a valley riddled with thorns, implies a less than inviting location; Underclough suggests a place buried under a gorge; Endlands evokes images of isolation and finality. Names of other sites also sound of desolation and menace: Sullom Wood, Fiendsdale Clough. This place is sublime, in the classic sense that phenomena that are chaotic, overpowering, and terrifying are also alluring and sometimes inescapable. Ultimately, the land both defines and intimidates the protagonists.

The Pentecost family name may initially seem a bulwark to the novel's portending geography. Yet before readers even meet the narrator and his family, they are presented with this old Endlands rhyme in the book's front matter just before the opening chapter:

> In the wink of an eye, as quick as a flea,
> The Devil he jumped from me to thee.
> And only when the devil had gone,
> Did I know that he and I'd been one.

The concept of the Christian Pentecost—the birth of the Church at the moment that the Holy Spirit enters into Christ's disciples, portrayed in some art as tongues of flames flickering above their heads—is recast as the supernatural aspect at the heart of the novel, that of the Devil, or some malicious spirit, entering a person and directing him or her toward some destructive action, before jumping into someone else to begin the cycle anew. Hurley uses the Pentecost family name in a deeply ironic sense when John tells the reader that, aside from Laurel, who is something of a born-again Christian, no one in his extended family

> had any interest in religion at all. The children of the three families might have been attending the Catholic primary in Underclough since it had been built, and gone through the Three-Cs of Confession, Communion and Confirmation, but only because it was easier than travelling miles to a different school. In the same way, a Christian burial was just a necessary bit of theatre that meant the dear departed could stay in the valley.

Another example of the families' detachment is found in John's casual dismissal of Halloween: "Halloween was a few days away and the village kids would soon be out trick-or-treating. . . . We'd never bothered with all that in the Endlands. We had Devil's Day instead."

Because the Pentecosts exist largely in their own world they have created their own rituals, like the titular celebration Devil's Day—a feast day held in the autumn during which the Devil is lured down off the moors, stuffed with food and wine until he falls asleep, and kept in the farmhouse until morning once the sheep have been safely pastured. What at first seems like an ancient practice only dates back to the end of World War I and was started by Joe Pentecost, the Gaffer's father and John's great-grandfather. Because they do not have the cultural anchor of faith, the Pentecosts and their neighbors are forced to re-create mythic history by establishing their own rituals to push back against the malign presence that lingers so tantalizingly out of sight for most of the novel and that seeks incursion into the world. It is this responsibility that the narrator, and later his wife, consciously take up, accepting as well the harrowing knowledge that comes with it.

Andrew Michael Hurley's sophomore effort succeeds on many levels. An elegantly written novel, *Devil's Day* is rich in Gothic and naturalistic imagery that captures the isolation, beauty, and otherworldliness of the British moors. A textbook example of the atmospheric "slow burn," Hurley's novel is characterized by expert pacing that effortlessly moves back and forth between time periods even as it moves fluidly toward a structurally satisfying and moving conclusion. *Devil's Day* further hones the literary craftmanship on display in Hurley's debut *The Loney* (2014). A fine example of literary horror, *Devil's Day* is highly recommended, and its author's future work should be of interest to critics and readers who seek to understand, not escape, the torments, natural and otherwise, of this world.

Realities Other Than the Ordinary

Peter Cannon

HENRY WESSELLS. *A Conversation Larger Than the Universe: Readings in Science Fiction and the Fantastic 1762–2017.* New York: The Grolier Club, 2018. $35.00 tpb. ISBN 978-1-605830-74-2.

On the evening of January 25, 2018, I attended the opening party for an exhibition at the Grolier Club, Manhattan's mecca for bibliophiles, of books and other printed materials drawn from the science fiction collection of Henry Wessells. A large crowd of well-dressed men and women thronged the second-floor gallery, where display cases held dozens of items, ranging from the first American edition of Mary Shelley's *Frankenstein* to Doc Savage paperback novels. As Michael Dirda has noted in a recent review, Wessells, a "raffish antiquarian bookseller," is "no literary snob."

In the introduction to the exhibit's catalogue—a collection of essays, some previously published, surveying the genre from its eighteenth-century Gothic origins to the present—Wessells states that he uses the terms "science fiction" and "the literature of the fantastic" interchangeably and that science fiction, fantasy, and horror share a common approach: "to make the reader experience realities other than our ordinary reality." He also makes it clear that his selections represent his personal enthusiasms. Among the illustrious names not on his list are Poe, Tolkien, Asimov, and Heinlein.

From chapter one, "Gothic Roots & Imaginary Voyages," I learned that the first English-language Gothic novel was *Longsword,* "a tale of menace and the betrayal of trust," written by Thomas Leland, an Irish clergyman and historian, and published in 1762. I was surprised, since I always thought that Horace Walpole's *The Castle of Otranto*, published two years later, was the first such novel. One of this volume's delights is discovering works one has never heard of.

In a later chapter, devoted to four distinguished twentieth-century women authors, I was surprised to come across Jean Rhys's *Wide Sargasso Sea* (1966), which tells the story of Bertha, the mad first wife of Mr. Rochester in Charlotte Brontë's nineteenth-century masterpiece *Jane Eyre*. How does this novel, which I've read, qualify as science fiction? Wessells includes it in the discussion because it's "a pioneering work." More to the point, he cites it as an example of *critical fiction,* in short "a writer's artistic response to another work of literature." Purists may quibble, but certainly this is a thought-provoking expansion of the genre.

The chapter covering the pre–World War I era, "Beautiful Books Before the Storm," reprints in color the opening page of the Doves Press edition of Shakespeare's *Hamlet* (1909). Wessells points out that *Hamlet* is a ghost story and comments on Shakespeare's influence on science fiction, but the reason for its inclusion appears to be mainly aesthetic. The page features a striking initial capital letter, an apple-green calligraphic W. Wessells clearly values typography and design. Indeed, this book, with its wide margins, ample space between lines, and elegant typeface, is itself an exemplar of the printer's art.

H. P. Lovecraft receives his own chapter, the only individual writer to be so honored. But only one chapter is devoted to a single work, John Crowley's fantasy *Little, Big,* which Wessells declares "my favorite work of fiction, a book I have read and reread many times." Crowley, appropriately, provides an appreciative foreword, "A Hatful of Adjectives for Henry Wessells." Even more appropriately, Crowley was one of the guests at the Grolier Club that festive evening. Not least of Wessells's virtues is his knack for making friends with the contemporary authors he admires, as evidenced by the inscriptions to him on a number of title pages illustrated in *A Conversation*. Long may he share his bookish interests with the rest of us!

About the Contributors

Michael J. Abolafia is an editor, writer, and archivist with a B.A. in English from Columbia University, and co-editor of *Dead Reckonings*.

James Arthur Anderson teaches writing and literature at Johnson & Wales University's North Miami Campus at the rank of professor. His latest book, *The Linguistics of Stephen King: Layered Language and Meaning in the Fiction,* was published by McFarland in 2017.

Leigh Blackmore is an Australian horror writer, critic, editor, occultist, and musician. He was the Australian representative for the Horror Writers of America and served as the second President of the Australian Horror Writers Association.

Ramsey Campbell is an English horror fiction writer, editor, and critic who has been writing for well over fifty years. He is frequently cited as one of the leading writers in the field. His web- site is www.ramseycampbell.com.

Peter Cannon is a senior editor at *Publishers Weekly,* assigning and editing the reviews in the Mystery/Thriller category. He is also the author of *H. P. Lovecraft,* a critical study in Twayne's U.S. Author Series, and other works related to Lovecraft.

Nathan Chazan is from Toronto, Canada. He is an under-graduate at Cornell University, majoring in classics. His writing has appeared in *Cleaver Magazine* and the *Cornell Daily Sun*.

Ryne Davis is a weird fiction enthusiast and collector from Walnut, Illinois.

Sam Gafford has been published in a wide variety of anthologies and publications. Recently he wrote *Some Notes on a Nonentity: The Life of H. P. Lovecraft,* a graphic-novel biography of Lovecraft.

Fiona Maeve Geist lives with her cat in WXXT country, where she freelances RPGs and writes short fiction. Her work has appeared in *Lamplight Quarterly,* CLASH Media, *Mothership* (RPG), and *Ashes and Entropy* (forthcoming).

J. T. Glover has published short fiction and nonfiction in *Best New Horror, Pseudopod, Postscripts to Darkness,* and *The Silent Garden,* among other venues. By day he is an academic librarian specializing in the humanities, and he studies literary horror, writers' research practices, and related topics.

Acep Hale is a magician, comedian, and writer who currently resides in Brooklyn, New York.

Alex Houstoun is a co-editor of *Dead Reckonings*.

S. T. Joshi is the author of such critical studies as *The Weird Tale* (1990), *H. P. Lovecraft: The Decline of the West* (1990), and *Unutterable Horror: A History of Supernatural Fiction* (2012). He has prepared corrected editions of H. P. Lovecraft's work for Arkham House and annotated editions of the weird tales of Lovecraft, Algernon Blackwood, Lord Dunsany, M. R. James, Arthur Machen, and Clark Ashton Smith for Penguin Classics, as well as the anthology *American Supernatural Tales* (2007).

Javier A. Martinez was managing editor of *Extrapolation* for fifteen years. A former department chair, college dean, and university provost, he is currently Professor of English in the Department of Literatures & Cultural Studies at The University of Texas Rio Grande Valley.

Charles D. O'Connor III is a thirty-five-year-old essayist and prose poet from Virginia Beach, Virginia. Lured into the boundless field of imagination by Rod Serling, he was soon hailed by the welcoming beacon of masterful weird authors such as H. P. Lovecraft, Clark Ashton Smith, and Algernon Blackwood. Now his literary tastes have been influenced by Lovecraft, along with the drive of Lord Dunsany and Clark Ashton Smith. He is also known for his collection of weird memorabilia.

Dr. Géza A. G. Reilly is a writer and critic with an interest in twentieth-century American genre literature. A Canadian expatriate, he now lives in the wilds of Florida with his wife, Andrea, and their cat, Mim.

Christopher Ropes is an author and musician who lives in New Jersey with his partner, their two children, and their cats. His work has been published by Dunhams Manor/Dynatox Industries and appeared in the first issue of *Vastarien: A Literary Journal*.

Darrell Schweitzer is an American writer, editor, and critic in the field of speculative fiction. Much of his focus has been on dark fantasy and horror, although he does also work in science fiction and fantasy. His latest book *The Dragon House*.

Joe Shea a.k.a. The joey Zone is an artist and illustrator. His work can be seen at www.joeyzoneillustration.com.

Donald Sidney-Fryer is a poet, historian, entertainer, and one of the foremost experts on the work of Clark Ashton Smith. His latest book, *Aesthetics Ho! Essays on Art, Literature and Theater,* was published by Hippocampus Press.

Hank Wagner is a respected critic and journalist. Among the many publications in which his work regularly appears are *Cemetery Dance* and *Mystery Scene*.

www.ingramcontent.com/pod-product-compliance
Lightning Source LLC
Chambersburg PA
CBHW071822020426
42331CB00007B/1582